Ketogenic Diet For Beginners

The Complete Keto Diet Cookbook For Beginners Delicious, Healthy, and Simple Keto Recipes For Everyone

Table of Contents

Introduction

As a newbie to the ketogenic diet, starting out can be so exciting, yet a little overwhelming. Mainly because there are very specific guidelines you have to follow in order to succeed on the ketogenic diet. But don't worry! With my cookbook in hand, I'll help you smoothly transition into ketosis so you can get the results you want.

Featuring everything from the science behind ketones to what you can actually eat on this diet, my detailed cookbook covers all the basic info you need to know about the Keto Diet. Oh, and let's not forget about my delicious Keto-friendly recipes that are also really easy to make!

Now, let's get into what makes the Keto Diet so different from the rest.

What is the Ketogenic Diet?

Put simply, the ketogenic diet is a low-carb diet that features a moderate amount of protein and is high in fat. After you follow the Keto diet for a while, your body will soon go into a metabolic state known as ketosis. While your body is in ketosis, your liver will start to produce ketones that will become the main source of energy for your body.

Now, why is everyone raving about this diet? Well, they're going crazy over the keto diet because it completely reverses how your body functions in the most natural way. It will even change your view on nutrition.

The keto diet is also based around the premise that your body works better as a fat burner than a sugar burner.

Fat vs. Sugar

After you enjoy a yummy, yet carb pack treat like a toasted bagel or sweet donut, your body will soon produce glucose and insulin.

Glucose happens to be the easiest molecule for your body to convert and use as a source of energy. This is the main reason why it's the preferred energy source for your body. While insulin is produced by your body to process the glucose in your bloodstream as it carries it around your body.

This may sound efficient, but the main problem with this process is that your body can only use so much glucose as its main energy source. Any extra glucose gets converted into fat so it can be stored instead.

When your body starts to runs low on glucose, it will then tell your brain that you need to grab a quick snack like candy or a bag of chips for more energy.

Now you can see how this dangerous cycle can lead to more body fat and health problems. The best way to stop this sugar cycle is to transform your body into a fat burner!

Once you're on Keto diet, you'll lower your carb intake enough so that your body can start to look for an alternative energy source – meaning ketosis! When your body is in this state of ketosis, it will produce ketones which occur when the liver breaks down fat.

If this is healthier for you, why isn't your body naturally break down fat in your liver? Well, when your body produces insulin, the ketosis process is blocked because insulin prevents the fat cells from entering the bloodstream. Instead, these fat cell are stored in your body.

So when you opt to lower your carb intake, your glucose and blood sugar levels will drop and eventually lower your insulin levels. This will allow fat cells to release the water they're storing (that means water weight) and have the fat cells enter your bloodstream and head to your liver.

As you can see this is the main goal of the keto diet. You just have to remember that you won't get into ketosis by starving your body, you can only enter this state by laying off the carbohydrates.

While you're in ketosis, you'll also see noticeable physical and mental benefits which I'll get into next!

How Can It Benefit you?

The right diet can change your life and the Keto Diet is no exception! I'm pretty sure you've heard or read stories from people raving about results they saw after going on the ketogenic diet.

When you switch over to the Keto Diet, you'll quickly see that it's much more than a low-carb diet. It's actually a new kind of lifestyle that offers tons of benefits – all of which I'll get into below.

Weight Loss

One of the most popular reasons why people look to change their diet is to lose weight. The keto diet happens to be the most effective way to lose weight since the diet will force your body to use fat as an energy source. So your body can easily burn all that unwanted fat and help you reach your weight goals.

Basically, your body will become a fat burning machine!

Better Control Over Your Blood Sugar

Unfortunately, there are a lot of people who suffer from diabetes due to their body's inability to handle insulin.

If you're one of them, being on the Keto diet will naturally lower your blood sugar levels because you're not eating a ton of carbs and producing extra glucose.

The keto diet is also a huge benefit to people who are pre-diabetic or have Type II diabetes.

Now, while you're on the ketogenic diet it will help you maintain healthier blood sugar levels and you'll have even more control over your everyday life.

Increase in Energy

Just above you learned that keto diet will help your body turn fat into an energy source. But, did you know that it can even increase your overall energy levels?

Since your body can only store so much glucose, when it eventually runs out your body also runs low on fuel (energy) and needs more. Carbs also cause your blood sugar levels to spike and when those levels drop you'll definitely feel the crash.

The keto diet will help provide you with a much more reliable energy source so you can be more energized throughout the day!

Mental Focus

Ever been under a mental fog all day? Well, that was probably a side effect from eating too many cloudy carbs that mess with your thinking. Now, when you start out on the ketogenic diet you'll experience an increase in your mental performance. In fact, a lot of people are switching to keto just for these benefits.

This is all thanks to those ketones that are a wonderful source of fuel for your brain!

Better Appetite Control

A diet full of empty carbs will leave you snacking all day long, but the Keto diet will keep you fuller. That's mainly because fats are naturally more satisfying and they end up leaving our bodies in a satiated state for much longer. This means no more cravings for random foods or feeling like you'll collapse if you don't eat something right away.

Epilepsy Treatment

The ketogenic diet has been used to treat people with epilepsy since the early 1900s. Even today, it's used to treat kids that suffer from uncontrolled epilepsy.

The keto diet offers those who are suffering from epilepsy a chance to take fewer medications, which is a huge benefit.

Cholesterol & Blood Pressure

Another area that the ketogenic diet has been shown to improve is triglyceride and cholesterol levels in your body.

These benefits include less toxic buildup in your arteries so that blood can easily flow throughout your body. Research also shows that a diet that is low in carbs and high in fat provide a huge increase in HDL (which is the good cholesterol) and a decrease in LDL (the bad kind of cholesterol).

Further studies have shown that low-carb diets improve blood pressure better than other diets.

Insulin Resistance

The main reason why people suffer from Type II diabetes is because of insulin resistance. The ketogenic diet helps these people lower their insulin levels down to a healthier range and get out of the high-risk group who are about to develop diabetes.

Acne

Now, the research on this specific benefit is limited, but people have reported that their skin is much clearer as a result of following a low-carb or ketogenic diet.

But an article by Italian researchers in 2012 dived into the potential benefits of a ketogenic diet for acne, which included the following:

- **Reduction in insulin levels:** When you suffer from elevated insulin levels it actually stimulates and increases the production of skin cells, sebum, and androgens – encouraging acne to spread and grow. A ketogenic diet will decrease insulin levels dramatically.
- **Anti-inflammatory Effects:** Inflammation really drives the growth of acne. A diet that is low in carbs like the ketogenic diet have been shown to reduce inflammation, which slows down acne.
- **Decrease in IGF-1:** Ketogenic diets decrease levels of IGF-1. Like insulin, IGF-1 increases sebum production and has been found to play a large role in acne. So, decreasing IGF-1 levels is definitely a good thing.

What Do I Eat on a Keto Diet?

Sadly, you can't eat whatever you want while you're on the ketogentic diet. With that being said, the keto diet isn't like any other diets out there. Because once you find yourself in ketosis, your cravings for anything you can't eat will soon disappear, and if they don't you'll have plenty of keto-friendly options.

You just need to remember the end of goal of the ketogenic diet is to get your body into a state of ketosis. To do this you'll need to drastically reduce your carb intake. This means being on the lookout for carbs that are not only in the junk foods you love, but in healthier foods as well.

Now let's get into exactly what you can and can't eat below.

Foods to Avoid

Grains and Carbs
Grains and carbs are a huge NO on the keto diet, so make sure you avoid the following:
- Pasta
- Rice
- Bread
- Barley
- Quinoa
- Cereal
- Pastries
- Wheat
- Buckwheat
- Beer
- Corn

Sugar
Sugar and products made with sugar will throw you out of ketosis so fast! Be vigilant and avoid them all.
- Cane sugar
- Agave syrup

- Ice creams
- Cakes
- Puddings
- Soft-drinks
- Artificial Sweeteners
- Juice
- Sports drinks
- Candy
- Chocolate
- Breakfast cereal

Fruits

Fresh, frozen or juiced, stay away from all fruit products that are high in carbohydrates. This includes the following:
- Tangerines
- Grapes
- Pineapples
- Mangos
- Papayas
- Dates
- Apples
- Bananas
- Oranges

Tubers

You'll have to avoid these starchy root vegetables from now on:
- Potatoes
- Yams
- Sweet potatoes
- Any kind of potato products

Low-Fat, Low-Carb Dairy Products

Dairy products that are really low-fat tend to have more carbs and sugar, while low-carb foods can contain artificial additives. So they aren't allowed on the Keto diet.
- Low-fat milk
- Low-fat yogurt
- Diet soda

Trans Fats, Refined Fats and Oils
Make sure you avoid these trans fats, refined fats and oils while on the Keto diet.

- Margarine
- Spreadable butter alternatives
- Safflower oil
- Sunflower oil
- Canola oil
- Cottonseed oil
- Soybean oil
- Grapeseed oil
- Corn oil

Processed Foods
Stay healthier by steering clear of these products and preservatives found in processed foods.

- Carrageenan - found in almond milk-based products
- Wheat gluten
- MSG - Added to whey protein products
- Sulphites - found in dried fruits and gelatin
- BPAs – they're often not labeled

Foods to Eat

Now that you know exactly what you can't eat on the Keto Diet, here's a quick rundown on what you can enjoy!

Meat and Protein
Remember to choose organic, pasture-raised, grass-fed meats when you can.

- Beef
- Poultry
- Pork
- Lamb
- Goat
- Organs
- Bacon
- Eggs

Seafood

Choose fresh, wild caught seafood, and try to avoid farm-raised fish.

- Shrimp
- Lobster
- Mussels
- Clams
- Crab
- Squid
- Octopus
- Tuna
- Salmon
- Mackerel
- Cod
- Halibut
- Mahimahi
- Catfish
- Oysters

Low-Carb Vegetables

Keto rule of thumb- stick to vegetables that grow above ground.

- Celery
- Asparagus
- Chives
- Radicchio
- Cauliflower
- Cucumber
- Radishes
- Broccoli
- Cabbage
- Endives
- Swiss chard
- Bok choy
- Lettuce
- Kale
- Spinach

Fats and Oils

Try to get most of your fat from natural sources, but you can also supplement it with saturated fats, monounsaturated fats, and polyunsaturated omega-3s.

- Olive oil
- Coconut oil
- Butter
- Ghee
- Avocado
- Macadamia nuts
- Lard
- Duck fat

Low-Sugar Fruits

Here are some fruits you can enjoy on the Keto Diet.

- Strawberries
- Blueberries
- Raspberries
- Cherries
- Mulberries
- Cranberries
- Avocados

High-Fat Dairy

Just make sure you buy full-fat dairy products such as the following:

- Heavy cream
- Hard cheeses like parmesan, Swiss, feta, and cheddar
- Soft cheeses like brie, mozzarella, Monterey Jack, and blue cheese
- Cream cheese
- Sour cream
- Full-fat yogurt
- Mayonnaise
- Cottage cheese

Nuts

You can definitely snack on a trail mix made with these nuts, but only in moderation.

- Macadamia nuts

- Pecans
- Brazil nuts
- Hazelnuts
- Walnuts
- Peanuts
- Pine nuts
- Almonds

Sweeteners

On the keto diet you can only use safe, low-glycemic sweeteners like these:
- Stevia
- Erythritol
- Monk fruit
- Any other kind of low-carb sweeteners

Keto Macros

Knowing how macros work is actually the key to being successful on the ketogenic diet. So, what are macros? Macros are the main source of calories in your everyday diet. There are three macros that you need to keep an eye on, which includes fats, protein and carbs.

Since the keto diet is high in fat, the majority of your daily calories comes from it. So the general ratio of macros that need to be followed in the keto diet is 70% fat, 25% protein, and 5% carbohydrates.

When you officially start your keto diet, your daily intake of net carbs shouldn't exceed 20g no matter what. Even if your recommended daily macro carb count is about 27g, you still need to stay at below 20g.

Tips for Eating Out

As you can see, the ketogenic diet has such a clear restriction on carbs and extra sugar that it can be really difficult to dine out. With that being said, below are a few tips you can follow that will make eating at a restaurant or fast food place a whole lot easier!

Do Some Research
Before you even head out to eat, do a quick search and find the restaurant menu.

You can do this by:

- Checking out the restaurant website
- Taking a look on Yelp
- Or Googling the restaurant's name followed by the keyword "menu."

From there you can decide on what keto-friendly meal you'll order at the restaurant. This way, when you actually get there, you'll know exactly what you're going to eat that's keto.

Stick with certain kinds of restaurants
Some restaurants are just more keto-friendly than others, and here are a few examples.

Good Keto restaurants:

- Steakhouses
- Mediterranean/Greek restaurants
- Middle Eastern restaurants
- Seafood restaurants
- Chinese restaurants
- Some BBQ joints

On the other hand, here are the restaurants you need to avoid on Keto:

- Pizzerias
- Sandwich shops
- Mexican restaurants
- Italian restaurants

You can definitely suggest any keto-friendly restaurants while going out for a meal with family and friends. Simply ask for their support and explain to them that eating at a certain restaurant will help you stay on track with your weight-loss and health goals.

Eat Before You Leave

I know the whole point of eating out is to, well eat out. But never go to a restaurant starving. It's one of the best ways to set back your diet.

So, go ahead and fill up on a light meal beforehand to make sure that you don't indulge in any unhealthy food choices.

Ask Questions

You're a customer who'll be paying and eating the food, so don't be afraid to ask questions!

Here are a few example questions you can ask to be on the safe side:

- If you're ordering any kind of seafood, fish, or meats, ask if it's breaded.
- Double check and ask if your dish comes with a sauce or extra toppings that aren't mentioned on the menu - a lot of sauces aren't Keto-friendly, which I'll get into more below.
- If you have any kind of food intolerance, ask if the restaurant can accommodate them before you go.

Eliminate the starch

You can't eat bread, pasta, potatoes or rice, so keep all that temptation far off your plate by taking these extra steps to replace them.

- If you're ordering an entrée meal, most restaurants will replace the starchy side with a salad or extra veggies if you ask.
- If you're in the mood for a sandwich or burger, most restaurants will actually wrap it in lettuce instead of serving the burger on a bun.
- If the restaurant doesn't substitute items, simply eliminate the unwanted item, regardless.

And if you feel like you have to explain yourself to the waiter, simply say you're on a restrictive diet.

Add healthy fats

Restaurant meals that are low in fat can be less satisfying without the carbs. However, this is an easy problem to fix!

- When you're ordering veggies or meat, ask for extra butter and melt it on top
- Skip the ranch and ask for olive oil and vinegar dressing to drizzle the oil on your salads and meal.
- Some restaurants tend to serve cheaper vegetable oils (full of omega 6 fat) instead of olive oil. To avoid this unhealthy oil many low-carb dieters carry a small bottle of olive oil with them.

Look out for certain sauces and condiments

Sauces like Béarnaise contain fat, while other condiments, like ketchup, contain a lot of carbs.

If you're not sure about what's in a sauce, just ask about the ingredients and avoid anything that contains sugar or flour. You can also ask to have the sauce on the side so you're in control of how much you want to add to the meal.

Choose your drinks wisely

Skip over the sodas and only drink water, sparkling water, coffee or tea while you're out.

If you want to drink an alcoholic beverage, select dry wine, champagne, light beer or spririts – with club soda or straight – which are all great low-carb options.

Think twice about dessert

Before you order dessert, ask yourself are you still hungry? If not, then order a nice cup of coffee or tea while everyone else finishes their sweets.

If you don't want to drink coffee because it's too late, then opt for decaf coffee or herbal tea. Now if you're still hungry and actually want dessert, then order a cheese plate or berries in heavy cream.

Tip! Sometimes adding cream or butter to your coffee is satisfying enough.

If necessary, get creative

Nothing's perfect, so you may need to improvise with the menu in front of you.

For example, if Spaghetti Bolognese is on the menu, you can ask them if they could serve you just the sauce in a bowl, with a large serving of sautéed vegetables on the side. You can enjoy both with a sprinkle of parmesan cheese too!

Or, maybe order two or three appetizers instead of a full main course. You can pair a salad with a yummy shrimp cocktail and a cheese plate to build a delicious low-carb dinner.

Don't Stress about it too much

When you do eat out with your friends and family, you may end up eating a little bit of sauce, dressing, glaze or a bit of breading. But don't beat yourself up over it!

It's just a little bit - but I'm definitely not giving you a free pass to "accidentally" eat a slice of pizza every time you go out.

Ketogenic Diet FAQ

So far, you've learned about how ketosis works, what you can eat and what you shouldn't, along with a few tips for eating out. Now check out my helpful FAQ section that will answer all your important questions!

How Long Does It Take To Get Into Ketosis?

Honestly, it does take time for your body to go into a ketosis state. But if you stay faithful to your new keto diet, you can be in Ketosis in around 2-7 days depending on your body type, what you're eating and activity level.

Tip! You can get into ketosis faster by exercising on an empty stomach, restrict your carb intake to just 20g or less a day, and keep note of your water intake.

Do I Need to Count Calories?

On the ketogenic diet you don't really need to worry too much about calories since the fats and proteins you eat will keep you full for a long period of time. If you exercise regularly, you need to be aware that exercising can put you into a greater calorie deficit than where you're suppose to be at. When this happens then you'll have to make it up with food.

Other than that, you just need to focus on eating properly, not going too far into a food deficit, and avoid snacking on foods that are bad for you.

How Can I Track My Carb Intake?

Using a helpful carb counting mobile app is one of the most common ways to track them. You can also find out your net carbs the old fashion way by subtracting your total fiber intake from your total carb intake.

Can I Eat Too Much Fat?

The short answer to this question is, yes, you can eat too much fat. Eating too much fat will definitely push you over the calorie deficit and it will turn into a calorie surplus. Most people find it really hard to over eat on a low-carb high fat diet, but it's still possible.

How Much Weight Will I Lose?

How much weight you lose depends 100% on you. For example, if you're exercising regularly then you will definitely speed up your weight loss results. Cutting out food that can stall your results like artificial sweeteners, wheat products and dairy can really help too.

Water weight loss is also common when you're first starting out since ketosis has a diuretic effect that can cause you to lose weight in a matter of days. Although this isn't fat, it shows that your body is beginning to become a fat burning machine.

How Do I Know When I'm in Ketosis?

One way is to pick up test strips that will give you a general idea of if you're in ketosis or not (since they tend to be pretty inaccurate).

Another reliable way to measure your ketone levels is with a blood ketone meter. If you do happen to get your hands on one, this is what the readings mean:

- **Light Ketosis**: 0.5 mmol/L – 0.8 mmol/L
- **Medium Ketosis**: 0.9 mmol/L – 1.4 mmol/L
- **Deep Ketosis** (this one is best for weight loss): 1.5 mmol/L – 3.0 mmol/L

I Just Started and I Don't Feel So Good. What Should I Do?

It's really common for people who start on the ketogenic diet to get headaches and "brain fogginess". This is mainly because ketosis has a diuretic effect on our body and you're losing electrolytes that you need to replace.

So, as you transition into ketosis, you need to stay hydrated and consume salt by eating a broth, other salty foods like deli meats and bacon, or salted nuts.

Can I Drink Alcohol on The Keto Diet?

You can drink alcohol, but you have to be careful since they do have hidden carbs. Wine, beer, and cocktails all have carbohydrates, so stick to clear liquors since they have less carbs.

Intro to Recipes

It's finally time to say farewell to carbs and hello to healthier, more fulfilling meals with the recipes that are waiting for you right below!

Just look through my recipe section and get ready to make everything from fluffy pancakes in the morning to a quick Italian style dinner and tasty jalapeño poppers that will be a hit with everyone.

Smoothies

Coconut Milk Strawberry Smoothie

Made with just four low carb ingredients, you'll be able to enjoy this keto-friendly Coconut Milk Strawberry Smoothie in just 2 minutes!

Prep Time: 2 Minutes
Total Time: 2 Minutes
Serves: 2

Ingredients:

- 1 cup strawberries frozen
- 1 cup unsweetened coconut milk
- 2 Tbsp. almond butter, smooth

Optional:

- 2 packets stevia

Directions:

1. Add the frozen strawberries, coconut milk and almond butter to your blender.
2. Pulse until smooth, for less than a minute.
3. Pour into a glass.
4. Enjoy!

Recipe Notes:

- To make two smoothies with a net carb count of 10g, reduce the amount of strawberries you use or opt for a coconut milk beverage to lower the carb count.

Macros Per Serving – Calories: 397 |Total Fat: 37g |Protein: 6g |**Net Carbs: 10g**

Blackberry Cheesecake Smoothie

Packed with protein and antioxidants, this delicious Blackberry Cheesecake Smoothie is a nutritious treat you can have for breakfast or as a snack.

Prep Time: 2 Minutes
Total Time: 2 Minutes
Serves: 1

Ingredients:

- ½ cup blackberries, fresh or frozen
- ¼ cup full-fat cream cheese or creamed coconut milk
- ¼ cup heavy whipping cream or coconut milk
- ½ cup water
- 1 Tbsp. MCT oil or extra virgin coconut oil
- ½ tsp. sugar-free vanilla extract or ¼ tsp. pure vanilla powder

Optional:

- 3-5 drops liquid Stevia extract or other healthy low-carb sweetener

Directions:

1. Add heavy whipping cream or coconut milk, cream cheese or creamed coconut milk, water, MCT oil or extra virgin coconut oil, vanilla extract or pure vanilla powder, and optionally a few drops of stevia into the blender.
2. Then add in the blackberries.
3. Pulse until smooth and frothy, for less than a minute.
4. Pour into a glass.
5. Enjoy!

Macros Per Serving – Calories: 515 |Total Fat: 53g |Protein: 6g |**Net Carbs: 6.7g**

Creamy Chocolate Smoothie

Filled with the healthy fats and nutrients you need, this very creamy Chocolate Smoothie is a great way to start your day!

Prep Time: 5 Minutes
Total Time: 5 Minutes
Serves: 1

Ingredients:

- ½ cup full-fat coconut milk or heavy cream
- ½ medium avocado to taste
- 1-2 Tbsp. cacao powder to taste
- ½ tsp. vanilla extract
- Pinch pink Himalayan salt or salt of choice
- 2-4 Tbsp. Swerve or sweetener of choice, to taste
- ½ cup ice, as needed
- Water, as needed

Optional Add-Ins:

- Chia seeds ground, add more water
- MCT oil
- Hemp hearts
- Collagen peptides
- Mint extract or extract of choice

Directions:

1. Add the coconut milk, avocado, cacao powder, vanilla extract, salt, sweetener along with the add-ins of choice to a blender.
2. Pulse until creamy smooth, adding a little water as needed.
3. Then add in ice and blend until thick and creamy – don't over-blend, or you'll lose the coldness and thickness.
4. Pour in a glass.
5. Enjoy!

Recipe Notes:

- Note that nutrition facts were estimated using 50g of avocado (about half a medium one avocado).

Macros Per Serving – Calories: 303 |Total Fat: 31g |Protein: 3g |**Net Carbs: 5.25g**

Blueberry Coconut Green Smoothie

In need of a green smoothie that doesn't taste so green? Then try our light and tasty Blueberry Coconut Smoothie with a yummy berry flavor.

Prep Time: 2 Minutes

Total Time: 2 Minutes

Serves: 2

Ingredients:

- ¼ cup sliced cucumber
- 1 cup fresh chopped kale
- 1 (13.5 oz. can) light coconut milk
- 1 cup frozen blueberries
- 1 cup water or ice
- 3 droppers full liquid vanilla stevia

Directions:

1. Add the sliced cucumber, kale, coconut milk, blueberries, ice or water and vanilla stevia to your blender.
2. Pulse on high until smooth, for less than a minute.
3. Pour into a glass.
4. Enjoy!

Macros Per Serving – Calories: 186 |Total Fat: 13g |Protein: 3g |**Net Carbs: 7g**

Peanut Butter Protein Smoothie

Your favorite creamy peanut butter and frozen mixed berries come together to create this healthy smoothie that tastes just like a classic PB&J.

Prep Time: 2 Minutes
Total Time: 2 Minutes
Serves: 1-2

Ingredients:

- ½ cup unsweetened almond milk
- ½ cup cottage cheese, low fat
- 1 Tbsp. natural peanut butter, no sugar added
- 1 cup ice
- 2 droppers full liquid stevia, toffee, vanilla or original

Optional:

- 1 scoop Whey Protein, of your choice

Optional topping:

- Cacao nibs
- Drizzle of peanut butter

Directions:

1. Add the almond milk, cottage cheese, natural peanut butter, ice, stevia and optional whey protein of your choice to your blender.
2. Pulse on high until smooth, for less than a minute.
3. Pour into a glass or glasses.
4. Enjoy.

Macros Per Serving (without Whey Protein) – Calories: 188 |Total Fat: 9g |Protein: 18g |**Net Carbs: 5g**

Blackcurrant Smoothie

Both delicious and sweet, there's no other taste quite like this Blackcurrant Smoothie.

Prep Time: 5 Minutes

Total Time: 5 Minutes

Serves: 1-2

Ingredients:

- ½ cup blackcurrants, fresh or frozen
- ¼ cup strawberries, 2-3 strawberries fresh or frozen
- ¼ cup coconut milk or heavy whipping cream
- ½ cup water
- 2 Tbsp. chia seeds, whole or powdered
- ½ vanilla bean or ½ tsp. sugar-free vanilla extract

Optional:

- 5-7 drops liquid Stevia extract or a different healthy low-carb sweetener

Directions:

1. Add the blackcurrant, strawberries, coconut milk or heavy whipping cream, water, chia seeds and vanilla bean into your blender.
2. Pulse on high until of smooth, for less than a minute.
3. Allow the smoothie to sit for 2-5 minutes.
4. Enjoy!

Macros Per Serving – Calories: 228|Total Fat: 17.3g |Protein: 5.1g |**Net Carbs: 8.7g**

Net Carbs in ½ cup of berries:

Strawberries: 4.1g |Raspberries: 3.3g |Blackberries: 3.1g |Blueberries: 8.9g (wild blueberries will have less carbs, ~ 7.3 g) |Blackcurrants: 4g

Cinnamon Roll Smoothie

Healthy and so delicious, this Cinnamon Roll Smoothie tastes just like a freshly baked treat.

Prep Time: 5 Minutes
Total Time: 5 Minutes
Serves: 1

Ingredients:
- 1 cup almond milk
- 2 Tbsp. vanilla protein powder, of your choice
- ½ tsp. cinnamon
- ¼ tsp. vanilla extract
- 3-4 tsp. stevia
- 1 tsp. flaxmeal
- 1 cup ice

Directions:
1. Add the almond milk, vanilla protein powder, cinnamon, vanilla extract, stevia, flaxmeal and ice in a blender.
2. Pulse on high until smooth and thick, for less than a minute.
3. Pour into a glass.
4. Enjoy!

Macros Per Serving – Calories: 145|Total Fat: 3.25g |Protein: 26.5g |**Net Carbs: 0.06g**

Chai Pumpkin Smoothie

Creamy pumpkin puree and exotic chai spices come together to make this filling Chai Pumpkin smoothie.

Prep Time: 5 Minutes
Total Time: 5 Minutes
Serves: 1-2

Ingredients:
- ¾ cup full-fat coconut milk
- 3 Tbsp. pumpkin puree
- 1 Tbsp. MCT oil, optional
- 1 tsp. loose chai tea
- 1 tsp. vanilla extract
- ½ tsp. pumpkin pie spice
- ½ fresh or frozen avocado

Directions:
1. Add the coconut milk, pumpkin puree, optional MCT oil, loose chai tea, vanilla extract, pumpkin pie spice and avocado.
2. Pulse on high until smooth and thick, for about 1 minute.
3. Pour into a glass.
4. Serve.

Recipe Notes:
- If you want to create your own pumpkin pie spice, simply mix together ¼ teaspoon ground cinnamon, 1/8 teaspoon ground ginger and 1/8 teaspoon ground nutmeg.

Macros Per 2 Serving – Calories: 726 |Total Fat: 69.8g |Protein: 5.5g |**Net Carbs: 11g**

Red Velvet Smoothie

Sweet and oh so addictive, this rich and chocolatey Red Velvet smoothie is great for breakfast or as a delightful snack.

Prep Time: 10 Minutes
Total Time: 10 Minutes
Serves: 1-2

Ingredients:

- 1 cup unsweetened vanilla almond milk
- ½ cup plain, nonfat Greek yogurt
- ¼ cup roasted beet puree
- ⅓ cup chocolate whey protein powder
- 1 Tbsp. unsweetened cocoa powder
- 2-4 drops of stevia, to taste

Directions:

1. Add the vanilla almond milk, Greek yogurt, roasted beet puree, chocolate whey protein, unsweetened cocoa powder and stevia to your blender.
2. Pulse on high until blended, for less than a minute.
3. Pour into a glass.
4. Enjoy!

Macros Per 2 Servings – Calories: 250 |Total Fat: 4.5g |Protein: 39g |**Net Carbs: 12g**

Citrus Green Smoothie

Creamy, sweet, and tart, this very green smoothie recipe with a touch of citrus is just what you need to start your day or enjoy as a healthy snack.

Prep Time: 5 Minutes
Total Time: 5 Minutes
Serves: 1

Ingredients:

- 8 oz. milk or non-dairy milk, of choice
- 1 scoop Micronutrients Greens Powder in Orange, brand of your choice
- 1 Tbsp. MCT oil
- 1 Tbsp. lemon juice
- 1 Tbsp. lime juice
- 1 handful ice
- 1 tsp. orange zest

Optional:

- 1/8 tsp. xanthum gum, if desired to make the smoothie thicker
- 1 handful of spinach, if desired

Directions:

1. Add the milk, micronutrient green powder in orange, MCT oil, lemon juice, lime juice, ice, optional xanthum, optional spinach and orange zest.
2. Pulse on high until smooth, for less than a minute.
3. Enjoy!

Macros Per Serving – Calories: 207 |Total Fat: 20g |Protein: 3g |**Net Carbs: 3g**

Breakfast

Pancakes

Light, fluffy, and really low in carbs. You'll want to have these keto-friendly pancakes every morning!

Prep Time: 3 Minutes
Cook Time: 5 Minutes
Total Time: 8 Minutes
Servings: 2
Yield: 8 small pancakes

Ingredients:

- 2 eggs large, separated
- 2 oz. heavy whipping cream
- 2 oz. almond flour, finely ground
- 1 tsp. unsalted butter
- 2 tsp. erythritol granulated
- ¼ tsp. baking powder, gluten free
- Pinch sea salt

Directions:

1. In a large mixing bowl, add the egg yolks, whipping cream, low carb sweetener, and salt, combine until the mixture is smooth, set aside.
2. In a small mixing bowl, add the almond flour with baking powder and then whisk it into the creamy egg mixture until it's smooth.
3. Using an electric mixer, and in a separate bowl beat the egg whites until soft peaks form, fold the egg whites into the batter.
4. In a large non-stick frying pan over medium heat melt the butter, making sure to evenly distribute the butter evenly.
5. Spoon in the batter to make the pancakes, using about 2 tbsp. per pancake.
6. Cook the pancakes for 3 minutes, or until lightly browned, and then gently flip each pancake and cook for an additional 2 minutes on the other side.
7. Repeat until all the batter is gone.
8. Serve!

Macros Per Serving – Calories: 339 |Total Fat: 30g |Protein: 12g |**Net Carbs: 4g**

Breakfast Stuffed Avocados

Enjoy a filling, delicious breakfast that includes a California avocados stuffed with eggs, bacon and sprinkled with cheese.

Prep Time: 10 Minutes
Cook Time: 10 Minutes
Total Time: 20 Minutes
Serves: 4
Yields: 8

Ingredients:

- 4 eggs
- 4 California avocados, halved and pitted
- 1/3 cup cooked bacon, crumbled
- 1/3 cup cheddar cheese shreds
- 1 Tbsp. butter
- Salt, to taste
- Pepper, to taste

Directions:

1. Preheat oven to broil on high.
2. Prepare the avocados by halving and pitting them with an Avocado Slicer or using a kitchen spoon.
3. Use the spoon to scoop out some of the avocado out to create a larger space for the filling, then set aside.
4. In a medium bowl, scramble the eggs, set aside.
5. In a small pan over medium heat, melt the butter and add the eggs, season with salt and pepper, cook until under done - a little runny is okay.
6. In a medium sized bowl, mix together the eggs with the cooked bacon.
7. Fill the avocados with a scoop of the eggs and bacon mixture, distributing it evenly between avocados.
8. Sprinkle with cheese.
9. Broil for 1-2 minutes until cheese is melted, keep an eye on them while they cook.
10. Once done, remove from oven and season if desired.
11. Enjoy!

Macros Per Serving – Calories: 244 |Total Fat: 20.3g |Protein: 6.8g |**Net Carbs: 5g**

Blueberries & Cream Crepes

Cream cheese and blueberries together make for a wonderful combination, especially when it's inside of a light crepe.

Prep Time: 10 Minutes
Cook Time: 30 Minutes
Total Time: 40 Minutes
Serves: 2
Yields: 6 crepes

Ingredients:
Crepe Batter:
- 2 large eggs
- 2 oz. cream cheese
- 10 drops liquid stevia
- ¼ tsp. cinnamon
- ¼ tsp. baking soda
- 1/8 tsp. sea salt

Filling:
- 60 grams blueberries
- 4 oz. cream cheese
- ½ tsp. vanilla extract
- 2 Tbsp. powdered erythritol

Directions:
1. In a bowl, combine the cream cheese and eggs and beat them with an electric hand mixer until smooth.
2. Add in the stevia, cinnamon, baking soda and sea salt, combine well.
3. In a nonstick pan over medium heat add in the butter or coconut oil to lightly grease the pan.
4. Once heated, pour in about ¼ cup of batter while swirling the pan to gently spread it the edges.
5. Cook until the edges begin to crisp about 3 minutes per crepe.
6. Loosen the edges with a spatula and then gently flip the crepe, repeat until all the batter is gone.
7. Prepare the filling by combining the cream cheese, vanilla extract and powdered erythritol in a small bowl, then beat with an electric hand mixer until smooth and creamy.

8. Add a small amount of the filling to the center of each crepe.
9. Add some fresh blueberries and wrap up the crepe.
10. Enjoy with extra cinnamon!

Macros Per Serving of 3 Crepes with Filling – Calories: 390 |Total Fat: 32g |Protein: 13g |**Net Carbs: 7g**

Cauliflower Hash Browns

These rich and buttery Cauliflower fritters are super easy to make on a busy morning, plus they pair so well with bacon.

Prep Time: 15 Minutes
Cook Time: 20 Minutes
Total Time: 35 Minutes
Serves: 4

Ingredients:

Cauliflower:
- 1 lb. raw cauliflower, grated
- 1 tsp. salt

Fritters:
- 3 large eggs
- 3 oz. onion chopped
- ½ cup almond flour
- ½ cup grated Parmesan cheese
- ½ tsp. baking powder
- 1 ½ tsp. lemon pepper

Directions:

1. Grate the cauliflower and place it into a colander, sprinkle with salt and mix thoroughly by hand, allow it to sit for 10 minutes.
2. Meanwhile, chop the onions and add them to a medium bowl.
3. Squeeze the water out of the cauliflower with clean hands.
4. Place the cauliflower into the medium bowl with the onions.
5. Add in the almond flour, cheese, baking powder and seasoning, mix thoroughly.
6. Then add the eggs and mix well to combine.
7. Place a frying pan over medium heat, once hot, add 1 Tbsp. of oil.
8. Using a 1/4 cup measuring cup, scoop out the cauliflower fritter batter and place into the hot skillet, cook for 3 minutes on both sides - only flipping the fritter when the bottom is well cooked.
9. Once done, drain the fritters on paper towels and repeat with any leftover batter.
10. Serve!

Macros Per Serving – Calories: 69 |Total Fat: 4g |Protein: 5g |**Net Carbs: 3g**

Macadamia Nut Granola

This wonderful low-carb granola recipe combines yummy macadamia nuts with coconut flakes, cacao nibs, freeze dried strawberries and raspberries to create flavorful granola bars.

Prep Time: 10 Minutes
Cook Time: 20 Minutes
Total Time: 30 Minutes
Serves: 8

Ingredients:
- 1 large egg white beaten
- 4 oz. raw macadamia nut
- 4 oz. raw sliced almonds
- 2 oz. raw cacao nibs
- 1 ½ oz. unsweetened flaked coconut
- ½ cup freeze-dried raspberries or strawberries
- 2 Tbsp. butter, ghee or coconut oil, melted
- ¼ cup low carb syrup like Sukrin gold fiber syrup
- 1 Tbsp. stevia or a different sugar alternative
- Pinch of salt

Directions:
1. Preheat oven to 325 degrees F.
2. Line a large sheet pan with parchment paper or foil.
3. With a food processor or a knife, chop the macadamia nuts into smaller pieces.
4. Chop the flaked almonds until they are the size of oats.
5. In a bowl, combine the macadamia nuts, almonds, cacao nibs, salt and butter, mix well to combine.
6. Add the syrup and mix thoroughly with a big spoon.
7. Then, add the egg whites and mix well to combine.
8. Pour the granola onto the baking sheet and evenly spread it out.
9. Bake for 15 to 25 minutes or just until it's fragrant and toasted on the bottom.
10. Allow the granola to cool completely before adding the flaked coconut and freeze-dried fruit.
11. Serve and store the leftovers in an air-tight container.

Macros Per Serving – Calories: 297 |Total Fat: 27g |Protein: 6g |**Net Carbs: 5g**

Breakfast Sausage with Guacamole Stacks

Stack your favorite breakfast ingredients – avocado, eggs and sausage, to create this quick and easy Sausage & Guac stacks.

Prep Time: 10 Minutes
Cook Time: 15 Minutes
Total Time: 25 Minutes
Serves: 2

Ingredients:

Quick Guacamole:

- 1 medium avocado
- ½ small white or yellow onion, chopped
- 2 Tbsp. fresh lime juice
- Salt, to taste
- Pepper, to taste

Stacks:

- 1-2 Tbsp. ghee, for frying
- 170g Italian sausage meat
- 2 large eggs
- Salt, to taste
- Pepper, to taste

Directions:

1. Prepare the guacamole by cutting the avocado in half and scooping it into a bowl.
2. Add the lime juice, onion, salt and pepper, then mash with a fork and set aside.
3. Create small patties with the sausage meat, wash hands and then set aside.
4. Greased a pan with half of the ghee and then place it over medium heat.
5. Once heated, add the sausage to the pan and cook for 2-3 minutes, then flip on the other side and cook for 1-2 more minutes, set aside.
6. Grease the pan with the remaining ghee and crack in the eggs, cook until the egg whites are cooked through and the egg yolks are still runny - If you use an egg mold then lower the heat since it will take longer to cook through.
7. Once done, top each patty with the prepared guacamole and the fried egg.
8. Season with salt and pepper to taste.
9. Enjoy!

Macros Per Serving – Calories: 509 |Total Fat: 43.9g |Protein: 20.1g |**Net Carbs: 4.4g**

Egg Casserole with Sausage

You'll love having this fluffy, delicious low carb sausage egg and cheese casserole in the morning. Plus, the squares are easy to reheat the next day for a quick on-the-go breakfast.

Prep Time: 10 Minutes
Cook Time: 30 Minutes
Total Time: 40 Minutes
Yields: 9 squares

Ingredients:
- 6 large eggs
- 1 lb. sausage bulk or chopped links
- 2 cups shredded cheese
- 1 cup coconut milk
- Non-stick cooking spray
- Salt, to taste
- Pepper, to taste

Directions:
1. Preheat oven to 350 degrees F.
2. In a pan over medium heat, brown the sausage until no longer pink.
3. In a bowl, beat the eggs and coconut milk together, season with salt and pepper.
4. Spray an 8×8 baking pan with non-stick spray.
5. Pour a thin layer of egg mixture into pan, covering the sausage.
6. Sprinkle with shredded cheese.
7. Pour the rest of the egg mixture evenly on top.
8. Bake for about 20-30 minutes, or until brown.
9. Allow it to cool for a bit and then serve.

Macros Per Serving – Calories: 381 |Total Fat: 32.3g |Protein: 20.8g |**Net Carbs: 1.5g**

Coconut Flour Porridge Breakfast Cereal

Match a quiet morning with this simple, warm coconut flour porridge that will be ready in minutes.

Prep Time: 2 Minutes
Cook Time: 5 Minutes
Total Time: 7 Minutes
Serves: 1

Ingredients:

- 2 Tbsp. coconut flour
- 2 Tbsp. golden flax meal
- ¾ cup water
- Pinch of salt
- 1 large egg, beaten
- 2 tsp. butter or ghee
- 1 Tbsp. heavy cream or coconut milk
- 1 Tbsp. your favorite sweetener

Optional:

- Fruits
- Nuts

Directions:

1. In a small pot over medium heat, add the coconut flour, golden flax meal, water and a pinch of salt, stir to combine.
2. Once the ingredients begin to simmer, turn it down to medium-low and whisk until it begins to thicken.
3. Remove the coconut flour porridge from heat.
4. Add the beaten egg, a half at a time, while whisking continuously.
5. Place back on the heat and then continue to whisk until the porridge thickens.
6. Remove from the heat and continue to whisk for about 30 seconds.
7. Then add the butter, cream and sweetener of your choice.
8. Garnish with your favorite toppings.

Macros Per Serving – Calories: 453 |Total Fat: 39g |Protein: 13g |**Net Carbs: 5.6g**

Shakshuka

Shakshuka is a delicious traditional Middle Eastern dish made with eggs poached in a flavorful tomato sauce, it's also low in carbs and ready in under 30 minutes!

Prep Time: 10 Minutes

Cook Time: 10 Minutes

Total Time: 20 Minutes

Serves: 2

Ingredients:
- 2 cups marinara sauce
- 2 chili pepper
- 8 eggs
- 2 oz. feta cheese
- ¼ tsp. cumin
- Salt, to taste
- Pepper, to taste
- Fresh basil, as garnish

Directions:
1. Preheat the oven to 400 degrees F.
2. Place a small skillet over medium heat, add a cup of the marinara sauce and some of the chopped chili pepper.
3. Allow the chili pepper to cook for about 5 minutes in the sauce.
4. Crack and gently lower the eggs into the marinara sauce.
5. Sprinkle feta cheese all over the eggs and then season with the salt, pepper and cumin.
6. Using an oven mitt, place the skillet into the oven and bake for about 10 minutes.
7. Once the eggs are cooked, but still runny, remove the skillet out with an oven mitt.
8. Chop the fresh basil and sprinkle it over the Shakshuka.
9. Enjoy!

Macros Per Serving – Calories: 490 |Total Fat: 34g |Protein: 35g |**Net Carbs: 4g**

California Chicken Omelette

Combine the freshest, low carb ingredients to make this amazing protein packed California Chicken Omelette that will keep you full for hours!

Prep Time: 10 Minutes
Cook Time: 10 Minutes
Total Time: 20 Minutes
Serves: 1

Ingredients:

- 4 eggs
- 4 slices bacon, cooked and chopped
- 2 oz. deli cut chicken
- ½ avocado
- 2 campari tomato
- 2 Tbsp. mayo
- 2 tsp. mustard

Directions:

1. Place a nonstick pan over medium heat.
2. In a small bowl, beat 2 eggs add them to a hot pan, pulling the sides of the eggs towards the center to cook the omelet.
3. Season the omelet with salt and pepper.
4. Once the eggs are halfway cooked about 5 minutes, add the deli cut chicken, bacon, sliced avocado and tomato along with a tablespoon of mayo and mustard to one half.
5. Fold the omelet over onto itself and cover with a lid, cook for an additional 5 minutes.
6. Enjoy!

Macros Per Serving – Calories: 415 |Total Fat: 32g | Protein: 25g| **Net Carbs: 4g**

Coconut Macadamia Bars

Take your breakfast to a whole new level with this fantastic coconut macadamia bars recipe!

Prep Time: 5 Minutes
Cook Time: 5 Minutes
Total Time: 10 Minutes
Serves: 5

Ingredients:
- .03 oz. macadamia nuts
- ½ cup almond butter
- ¼ cup coconut oil
- 6 Tbsp. unsweetened shredded coconut
- 20 drops stevia drops

Directions:
1. In a food processor or by hand, crush the macadamia nuts.
2. In a bowl, combine the almond butter, coconut oil and shredded coconut.
3. Add the macadamia nuts and the stevia drops, mix thoroughly.
4. Pour the batter into a 9x9 parchment paper lined baking dish.
5. Refrigerate the bars overnight.
6. The following day slice and enjoy.

Recipe Notes:
- To make crunchier bars, store the bars in the freezer.

Macros Per Serving – Calories: 425 |Total Fat: 42g |Protein: 6g |**Net Carbs: 4g**

Appetizers & Snacks

Buffalo Chicken Strips

Quick and easy, add some heat to your party with these buffalo chicken strips that are both spicy and delicious! Remember to serve them up with keto-friendly ranch dressing and celery sticks.

Prep Time: 5 Minutes
Cook Time: 20 Minutes
Total Time: 30 Minutes
Serves: 4

Ingredients:
- ½ tsp. garlic powder
- ½ tsp. paprika
- ½ tsp. chili powder
- 1/8 tsp. black pepper
- ½ Tbsp. oil
- 8 strips chicken tenderloin
- ¼ cup Frank's Hot Sauce or your favorite hot sauce
- 4 celery stalks, trimmed to 4-inch strips

Optional:
- ½ cup Keto-friendly ranch dressing

Directions:
1. In a bowl, combine the garlic powder, paprika, chili powder and black pepper.
2. Season chicken with the spice mix, tossing evenly to coat the chicken.
3. In a large non-stick sauté pan over medium-high heat, add half of the oil.
4. Once heated, add half of the chicken and cook until golden, about 3-4 minutes, then turn chicken and cook until the center is no longer pink, set aside and pat the chicken dry.
5. Repeat the previous step with remaining oil and chicken.
6. Pour the hot sauce over the chicken, tossing well.
7. Serve with celery sticks and ranch dressing if desired.

Macros Per Serving – Calories: 111 |Total Fat: 2g |Protein: 21g |**Net Carbs: 1g**

Stuffed Jalapeño Peppers

The mouth-watering combination of crunchy bacon and creamy cheese makes these Stuffed Jalapeño Pepper the perfect snack or appetizer.

Prep Time: 10 Minutes
Cook Time: 25 Minutes
Total Time: 35 Minutes
Yields: 20 Halves

Ingredients:

- 8 - 10 jalapeño peppers halved lengthwise, stems, seeds and membranes removed
- 6 oz. cream cheese
- 0.05 lb. Monterey jack cheese, or cheese of your choice
- 1 Tbsp. garlic powder
- 1 Tbsp. onion powder

Directions:

1. Preheat the oven to 350 degrees F.
2. Lightly grease a baking sheet.
3. In a bowl, combine the cream cheese, garlic and onion powder.
4. Spread the cheese mixture into the jalapeños.
5. Cut the Monterey Jack cheese into slices and place it on top of the jalapeños.
6. Place them on the baking sheet.
7. Bake in the oven for 25 minutes until the top of the cheese is golden.
8. Eat and enjoy!

Macros Per Serving – Calories: 52 |Total Fat: 4g |Protein: 2g |**Net Carbs: 1g**

BLT Dip

Any fan of the classic bacon, lettuce and tomato sandwiches will fall for this creamy, keto-friendly BLT dip!

Prep Time: 10 Minutes
Cook Time: 10 Minutes
Total Time: 20 Minutes
Serves: 12

Ingredients:

- 1 lb. of bacon, cooked and chopped or 5 oz. of bacon crumbles
- 8 oz. cream cheese
- ¼ cup mayo
- ¼ cup sour cream
- ¼ cup shredded cheddar
- 1 tsp. onion powder
- 1 tsp. dried minced garlic
- ½ tsp. smoked paprika or regular
- A pinch of salt
- 1 cup chopped lettuce
- 1 cup chopped tomato, squeeze out the juice after chopping
- Fresh veggies to dip

Directions:

1. In a deep-dish pie plate, combine the 1/3 of the bacon with the cream cheese, sour cream, mayo, cheddar, and seasonings.
2. Top with the lettuce, tomato, and the rest of the bacon.
3. Serve with fresh veggies to dip.

Macros Per Serving – Calories: 278 |Total Fat: 26 g |Protein: 6g |**Net Carbs: 2g**

Garlic Parmesan Wings

Drenched in a buttery garlic Parmesan sauce, these crispy oven baked wings are the perfect low-carb appetizer everyone will enjoy!

Prep Time: 15 Minutes
Cook Time: 50 Minutes
Total Time: 1 Hour 5 Minutes
Serves: 8

Ingredients:

- 3 lbs. chicken wings
- 1 ½ Tbsp. baking powder
- Salt and pepper
- ¼ cup salted butter
- 4 cloves garlic minced
- 2 tsp. dried parsley
- Pinch red pepper flakes
- ½ ounce grated Parmesan about ½ cup
- Fresh chopped rosemary or parsley

Directions:

1. Preheat oven to 250 degrees F.
2. Place a baking rack over a baking sheet lined with foil, brush the rack with oil to prevent the chicken from sticking.
3. Pat wings dry and place in a plastic bag.
4. Add the baking powder, salt, and pepper and seal the bag, shake to coat.
5. Lay the wings in a single layer on the prepared baking rack and bake in lower third of oven for 30 minutes.
6. Increase oven temperature to 425 degrees F and move baking sheet to upper third of oven, continue to bake for another 20 to 30 minutes, until crispy, then transfer to a large bowl.
7. In the meantime, melt the butter in a microwaveable safe bowl or in a saucepan.
8. Add the garlic, parsley and pepper flakes, pour over the chicken wings and sprinkle with the Parmesan, tossing well to coat, sprinkle with chopped parsley, and sprinkle with additional salt and pepper to taste.
9. Serve immediately with your favorite dipping sauce.

Macros Per Serving – Calories: 386 |Total Fat: 28.15g |Protein: 30.62g |**Net Carbs: 1.30g**

Loaded Cauliflower

Made with butter, sour cream, chives, cheddar cheese and bacon, this loaded cauliflower recipe makes for the ultimate low carb comfort food!

Prep Time: 10 Minutes
Cook Time: 10 Minutes
Total Time: 20 Minutes
Serves: 4

Ingredients:

- 1 lb. cauliflower, cut into florettes
- 4 oz. sour cream
- 1 cup grated cheddar cheese
- 2 slices cooked bacon crumbled
- 2 Tbsp. snipped chives
- 3 Tbsp. butter
- ¼ tsp. garlic powder
- Salt, to taste
- Pepper, to taste

Directions:

1. Cut the cauliflower into florettes and add them to a microwave safe bowl.
2. Add 2 Tbsp. of water and cover with cling film, microwave for 5 to 8 minutes, depending on your microwave, until completely cooked and tender.
3. Drain any excess water and allow it to sit uncovered for 1 to 2 minutes.
4. Add the cauliflower to a food processor and process until fluffy.
5. Add in the butter, garlic powder, and sour cream and process until the consistency resembles mashed potatoes.
6. Remove the mashed cauliflower to a bowl and add in most of the chives, reserving some as a garnish.
7. Add half of the cheddar cheese and mix by hand, season with salt and pepper.
8. Top the loaded cauliflower with the remaining cheese, chives and bacon.
9. Put the bowl back into the microwave to melt the cheese or place the cauliflower under the broiler for a few minutes.
10. Enjoy!

Recipe Note:

- Alternately, you can also steam your cauliflower. You may need to squeeze a little water out of the cauliflower after its cook.

Macros Per Serving – Calories: 199 |Total Fat: 17 g |Protein: 8g |**Net Carbs: 3g**

Avocado Fries

Seasoned to perfection and super crunchy, these avocado fries are only made with four ingredients and are ready in just 15 minutes!

Prep Time: 10 Minutes

Cook Time: 15 Minutes

Total Time: 25 Minutes

Serves: 2

Ingredients:

- 1 large avocado not too ripe
- ½ cup almond meal
- 1 tsp. cajun seasoning
- ¼ cup almond milk
- Non- stick baking sheet

Directions:

1. Preheat oven to 450 degrees F.
2. Cut the avocado lengthwise and twist halves to separate, removing the pit and peeling skin off.
3. Then cut the avocado into wedges.
4. In a shallow bowl, add the almond milk.
5. In a separate bowl, combine the almond meal and cajun seasoning.
6. Dip avocado slices in almond milk then press them into the almond meal to thoroughly coat the avocado slices – you can also pour the almond meal over the avocado with a spoon.
7. Place the avocado fries on nonstick baking sheet.
8. Bake for 15 to18 minutes until lightly golden.
9. Remove from oven and allow them to cool for 1 to 2 minutes.
10. Serve!

Recipe Notes:

- To make a quick dipping sauce, add ¼ cup mayonnaise with 2 Tbsp. plain, full-fat Greek yogurt and 1 Tbsp. buffalo sauce in a bowl, mix thoroughly.

Macros Per Serving – Calories: 206 |Total Fat: 19.3g |Protein: 3.8g |**Net Carbs: 2.5g**

Caprese Meatballs

Savory with just a hint of spiciness, these very crispy meatballs are filled with mozzarella and can either be topped with marinara sauce or served on party skewers.

Prep Time: 10 Minutes
Cook Time: 20 Minutes
Total Time: 30 Minutes
Yield: 16 meatballs

Ingredients:
- 1 lb. ground turkey
- 1 egg
- ¼ cup almond flour
- ½ tsp. salt
- ¼ tsp. ground black pepper
- ½ tsp. garlic powder
- ½ cup shredded whole milk mozzarella
- 2 Tbsp. sun dried tomatoes, chopped
- 2 Tbsp. fresh basil, chopped
- 2 Tbsp. olive oil for frying

Directions:
1. In a medium bowl, add the ground turkey, egg, almond flour, salt, ground black pepper, garlic powder, mozzarella, sun dried tomatoes and fresh basil, mix thoroughly.
2. Form into 16 meatballs.
3. Place a large nonstick sauté pan over medium heat, add in the olive oil.
4. Once heated, add in the meatballs about 1 inch apart, cook over low/medium heat for 3 minutes per side or until thoroughly cooked - the cheese will melt out so be careful not to burn them or turn the heat down if they're browning too quickly.
5. Serve alone, with marinara sauce or on skewers between fresh mozzarella, basil leaves, and cherry tomatoes.
6. Enjoy!

Macros Per Serving (4 meatballs) – Calories: 312 |Total Fat: 24g |Protein: 24g |**Net Carbs: 2g**

Coconut Chocolate Chip Cookies

A little crispy and a little chewy, these low carb chocolate chip cookies will definitely satisfy your sweet tooth.

Prep Time: 15 Minutes
Cook Time: 15 Minutes
Total Time: 30 Minutes
Yields: 20

Ingredients:
- 1 ¼ cups almond flour
- ¾ cups finely shredded unsweetened coconut
- 1 tsp. baking powder
- ½ tsp. salt
- ½ cup butter softened
- ½ cup Swerve Sweetener
- ½ tsp. vanilla extract
- 1 large egg
- 1/3 cup sugar-free chocolate chips
- 2 tsp. Yacon syrup or molasses, optional

Directions:
1. Preheat the oven to 325 degrees F.
2. Line a large baking sheet with parchment paper or a silicone liner.
3. In a medium bowl, whisk together the coconut shreds, almond flour, baking powder and salt.
4. In a large bowl, mix the cream butter with Swerve Sweetener and molasses.
5. Beat in the vanilla and egg until well combined.
6. Beat in flour mixture until the dough is well mixed.
7. Stir in sugar-free chocolate chips.
8. Shape the dough into 1 ½-inch balls and place them 2 inches apart on prepared baking sheet.
9. Press each ball with the heel of your hand to ¼ inch thickness.
10. Bake for 12 to 15 minutes, until it begins to brown and is barely firm to the touch.
11. Remove from oven and allow to cool completely on the pan.
12. Serve!

Macros Per Serving – Calories: 238 |Total Fat: 21.59 g |Protein: 4.39g |**Net Carbs: 4.81g**

Peanut Butter Cheesecake Bites

Tiny and sweet, these lil' bites of cheesecake are pack with chocolate peanut butter cup flavor you'll absolutely love!

Prep Time: 5 Minutes
Freeze Time: 50 Min- 1 Hour
Total Time: 55 Min- 1 Hour to 5 Minutes
Yields: 6 Peanut Butter Cheesecake Bites

Ingredients:

- 8 oz. cream cheese, softened
- ¼ cup powdered erythritol
- 1 tsp. vanilla extract
- ¼ cup heavy whipping cream
- ¼ cup peanut butter, sugar-free
- ¾ cup sugar-free chocolate
- 2 tsp. coconut oil

Directions:

1. In a bowl, combine the cream cheese, erythritol, and heavy whipping cream until smooth.
2. Mix in the peanut butter and vanilla extract until fully combined, set aside.
3. Melt the chocolate and mix with coconut oil.
4. Brush silicone cups with the chocolate coconut oil mixture and place into the freezer for 5 minutes.
5. Repeat previous step and freeze again for 10 minutes.
6. Place a full spoonful(s) of cheesecake fluff into cup and freeze for 15 minutes.
7. Top the cups with chocolate to cover cheesecake fluff.
8. Then freeze for 20 minutes covered or refrigerate for 1 hour.
9. Enjoy!

Recipe Notes:

- Store them in the fridge after they initially set. And if you store the peanut butter cheesecake bites in the freezer allow them to set 10-15 minutes to thaw before eating.

Macros Per Serving – Calories: 233 |Total Fat: 22g |Protein: 4g |**Net Carbs: 4g**

Cranberry Chocolate Chip Granola Bars

Full of tart dried cranberries and chocolate chips, these Granola Bars definitely make for a delicious treat at snack-time!

Prep Time: 10 Minutes
Cook Time: 25 Minutes
Total Time: 35 Minutes
Yields: 16 bars

Ingredients:

- 1 cup flaked coconut
- 1 cup sliced almonds
- ½ cup pecan halves
- ½ cup sunflower seeds
- 1/3 cup dried unsweetened cranberries chopped
- 1/3 cup sugar-free chocolate chips
- ½ tsp. salt
- ½ cup butter
- 2 tsp. Yacon syrup or 1 Tbsp. Sukrin gold fiber syrup
- ½ cup powdered Swerve Sweetener
- ½ tsp. vanilla extract

Directions:

1. Preheat the oven to 300 degrees F.
2. Line a 9x9 or 8x8 inch pan with parchment paper with a little of the parchment overhanging the sides for easy removal.
3. In a food processor, combine the coconut, almonds, pecans, and sunflower seeds, process on high until the mixture resembles coarse crumbs in texture.
4. Transfer the mixture to a bowl and then stir in the cranberries, chocolate chips and salt.
5. In a medium saucepan over low heat, melt the butter with the Yacon or the fiber syrup.
6. Once melted, whisk in the powdered sweetener until smooth, stir in the vanilla extract.
7. Then stir the butter mixture into the nut and coconut mixture until thoroughly combined.
8. Press evenly into the bottom of prepared baking pan by using the flat-bottomed glass or measuring cup to press and compact it as much as possible.
9. Bake for 25 minutes, or until the edges turn golden brown.

10. Allow the granola to cool completely in the pan and then lift them out with the parchment paper.
11. Use a very sharp knife and cut them into bars, cutting straight down.
12. Serve!

Macros Per Serving – Calories: 179|Total Fat: 16 g |Protein: 3g |**Net Carbs: 4g**

Soft Mini Pretzel

Chewy and buttery, these easy to make bite-sized pretzels are perfect for a party or as a quick snack with yummy dipping sauce.

Prep Time: 15 Minutes
Cook Time: 14 Minute
Total Time: 29 Minutes
Yields: 6 pretzels

Ingredients:
- 2 cups blanched almond flour
- 1 Tbsp. baking powder
- 1 tsp. garlic powder
- 1 tsp. onion powder
- 3 large eggs, divided
- 3 cups shredded low moisture mozzarella cheese
- 5 Tbsp. cream cheese
- Coarse sea salt, for topping

Directions:
1. Preheat oven to 425 degrees F.
2. Line a rimmed baking sheet with parchment paper.
3. In a medium mixing bowl, combine the almond flour, baking powder, garlic powder, and onion powder, mix well until combined.
4. In a small bowl, prepare the egg wash by whisking one of the eggs with a fork.
5. In a large microwave safe mixing bowl, combine the mozzarella cheese and cream cheese and microwave for 1 minute and 30 seconds, remove from microwave and stir to combine.
6. Then return to microwave for 1 additional minute, mix well until combined.
7. Prepare the dough in mixing bowl by adding the remaining 2 eggs and the almond flour mixture, mix until all ingredients are well incorporated - If the dough is too stringy and unworkable, place it back in the microwave for 30 seconds to soften and continue to mix.
8. Divide the dough into 6 equal portions.
9. Roll each portion into a long, thin piece that resembles a breadstick.
10. Fold each one into the shape of a pretzel.
11. Brush the top of each pretzel with the egg wash and sprinkle coarse sea salt over top.
12. Bake on the middle rack for 12 to 14 minutes or until golden brown.
13. Serve alone or with dipping sauce of your choice!

Macros Per Serving – Calories: 449 |Total Fat: 35g |Protein: 28g |**Net Carbs: 6g**

Strawberry Cheesecake Popsicles

Cool down on a hot day with these creamy sugar-free strawberry cheesecake popsicles that are still sweet!

Prep Time: 15 Minutes
Chill Time: 4 Hours
Total Time: 4 Hours 15 Minutes
Yields: 12 popsicles

Ingredients:

- 8 oz. cream cheese softened
- 1 cup cream
- 1/3 cup powdered Swerve Sweetener
- ¼ tsp. stevia extract or monk fruit extract
- 1 Tbsp. lemon juice
- 2 tsp. lemon zest
- 2 cups fresh strawberries chopped, divided

Directions:

1. Add the cream cheese into a food processor and process until smooth.
2. Then add the cream, powdered Swerve sweetener, lemon juice, lemon zest and stevia extract or monk fruit extract, process until well combined.
3. Add in 1 ½ cups of the strawberries and process until almost fully smooth, then stir in remaining chopped strawberries.
4. Pour the mixture into popsicle molds and add in the wooden popsicle sticks about 2/3 of the way into each popsicle.
5. Freeze for at least 4 hours.
6. To unmold, run the mold under hot tap water for 20 to 30 seconds, and then gently twist stick to release them.
7. Enjoy!

Macros Per Serving – Calories: 122 |Total Fat: 12g |Protein: 2g |**Net Carbs: 2g**

Almond Butter Fudge Bars

Make these delightful almond butter fudge bars for the whole family or enjoy them as a quick lunch-time snack!

Prep Time: 25 Minutes
Cook Time: 10 Minutes
Total Time: 35 Minutes
Yields: 8

Ingredients:

- 1 cup almond flour
- ½ cup unsalted butter, melted and divided
- 6 Tbsp. powdered erythritol, divided
- ½ tsp. ground cinnamon
- ¼ cup heavy cream
- ½ cup almond butter
- ½ tsp. vanilla extract
- 1/8 tsp. xanthan gum
- 1 oz. 80% dark chocolate or sugar-free chocolate chips

Directions:

1. Preheat the oven to 400 degrees F.
2. Line a 9x13 inch or similar baking dish with parchment paper.
3. Whisk together the almond flour, ¼ cup melted butter, 2 Tbsp. powdered erythritol and cinnamon until well-combined.
4. Spread the mixture on the lined baking dish.
5. Bake for 10 minutes until golden brown.
6. Whisk together the heavy cream and almond butter with the remaining butter and 4 Tbsp. powdered erythritol in a mixing bowl.
7. Add the vanilla and xanthan gum, blending until well-combined.
8. Spread the fudge mixture over the cooled almond flour base.
9. Sprinkle with roughly chopped dark chocolate or sugar-free chocolate chips.
10. Freeze overnight and then slice the fudge into 8 bars.
11. Serve.

Macros Per 1 Bar – Calories: 235 |Total Fat: 24g |Protein: 4.5g |**Net Carbs: 2g**

Candied Toasted Coconut Cashews

Super addictive and sugar free, you'll enjoy snacking on these candied cashews mixed with toasted coconut!

Prep Time: 10 Minutes
Cook Time: 45 Minutes
Total Time: 55 Minutes
Serves: 2

Ingredients:
- 3 cups unsalted cashews
- 1 cup granulated monk fruit sweetener
- 1 Tbsp. cinnamon
- ¼ cup water
- 1 tsp. vanilla extract
- ½ tsp. salt
- ½ cup toasted coconut flakes

Directions:
1. Preheat oven to 250 degrees F.
2. Line a large baking dish or tray with parchment paper and set aside.
3. In a large mixing bowl, add the cashews, cinnamon, and salt, set aside.
4. In a microwave-safe bowl or stovetop, melt the monk fruit sweetener with water.
5. Pour it over the cashews and mix until all cashews are evenly coated.
6. Spread the cashews in an even layer.
7. Bake for 45 minutes, stirring occasionally.
8. Once the cashews have begun to crystallize, remove and allow them to cool for 1-2 minutes, before stirring again to avoid clusters from forming.
9. Allow them to cool completely before coating with an extra tbsp or two of monk fruit sweetener.
10. Once they are cooled, toss in the coconut flakes.
11. Serve!

Recipe Notes:
- Keep the remaining cashews in a sealed jar or container. They can be kept for up to two months or in the freezer for up to 6 months.

Macros Per Serving – Calories: 99 |Total Fat: 5 g |Protein: 6g |**Net Carbs: 1g**

Fish & Seafood

Easy Salmon Cakes

Quickly make these flaky and flavorful Salmon cakes for lunch or dinner when you're in a hurry!

Prep Time: 5 Minutes
Cook Time: 10 Minutes
Total Time: 15 Minutes
Serves: 2

Ingredients:
Salmon cakes:

- 2 x 5 oz. pouch of pink salmon or cans, drained well
- 1 egg
- ½ jalapeño, finely chopped
- 2 Tbsp. sarayo or plain mayo
- 2 Tbsp. red onion, finely diced
- ¼ tsp. garlic powder
- ¼ tsp. chili powder
- Salt, to taste
- Pepper, to taste
- 1 Tbsp. avocado oil

Optional:

- ¼ cup finely ground pork rinds

Avocado cream sauce:

- 1 avocado
- ¼ cup sour cream
- 3 Tbsp. cilantro
- 1-2 Tbsp. avocado oil (to thin)
- 1-2 tsp. Water, to desired thickness
- Juice of half lemon
- Salt, to taste
- Pepper, to taste

Directions:

1. Prepare the cream sauce by adding the avocado, sour cream, cilantro, avocado oil, water, lemon juice, salt and pepper, blend until to smooth, set aside.
2. In large bowl, combine the salmon, egg, jalapeño, sarayo, red onion, ground pork rinds, salt and pepper.

3. Form 4 large or 5-6 patties with the mixture.
4. In a nonstick skillet over medium heat, drizzle oil and cook patties cook for 4 to 5 minutes until each side is golden brown and crispy.
5. Serve with avocado cream sauce.
6. Enjoy!

Macros Per 2 Servings – Calories: 542 |Total Fat: 50g |Protein: 10g |**Net Carbs: 4g**

Lemon Baked Cod with Parmesan Cheese

Baked in Parmesan cheese and butter, this cod recipe is such an easy weeknight dinner!

Prep Time: 15 Minutes
Cook Time: 15 Minutes
Total Time: 30 Minutes
Serves: 3

Ingredients:

- 1 ½ lb. cod fillets, thawed if frozen
- ¾ cup finely grated parmesan cheese
- 1 lemon, zested and juiced
- 4 cloves garlic, minced
- 4 Tbsp. salted butter, melted
- 1 Tbsp. fresh parsley, chopped
- 1 tsp. paprika
- Salt, to taste
- Pepper, to taste

Directions:

1. Preheat the oven to 400 degrees F.
2. Pat the cod fillets dry using paper towels, removing the bones if any.
3. In a shallow bowl, add the melted butter and minced garlic, stir together until well combined, set aside.
4. In another shallow bowl, add the Parmesan and paprika, stir together until well combined, set aside.
5. Prepare a baking dish large enough for all cod fillets to sit in a single layer and line the dish with parchment paper.
6. Prepare one fillet at a time by dipping it into the melted butter and flip to coat all sides, then cover it with the parmesan mixture on all sides, and place it onto the lined baking dish.
7. Repeat with the other cod fillets and lay them evenly on the baking dish, sprinkle any remaining parmesan on top of the fillets, pressing down to adhere.
8. Sprinkle the parsley and half of the lemon zest on top of the cod fillets.
9. Bake for 15 minutes, until the cod is cooked through and easily flakes with the use of a fork.
10. Spoon the lemon juice on top of the cod, about 2 Tbsp.
11. Sprinkle the remaining lemon zest on top and season with salt and pepper to taste.
12. Enjoy!

Macros Per Serving – Calories: 410 |Total Fat: 20g |Protein: 49g |**Net Carbs: 1.5g**

Salmon Tzatziki with Cucumber Noodles

Ready in just 30 minutes, this Salmon tzatziki paired with fresh cucumber noodles is the ideal meal on a weeknight!

Prep Time: 10 Minutes
Cook Time: 20 Minutes
Total Time: 30 Minutes
Serves: 4

Ingredients:

For the Tzatziki Sauce:

- 140g Greek-style yogurt
- 1 Tbsp. extra virgin olive oil
- 1 Tbsp. white wine vinegar
- 1 Tbsp. lemon juice
- 1-2 cloves garlic, grated or ran through a press
- 1 tsp. fresh dill or ¾ tsp. dried
- Kosher salt, to taste
- 1 cucumber spiralized or grated

For the Salmon:

- 2 salmon fillets, about 5 oz. each, skins on
- 1 Tbsp. extra virgin olive oil
- 1 tsp, freshly grated lemon zest
- 2 cloves garlic, grated or press
- Kosher, to taste
- Freshly ground pepper, to taste

Directions:

For the Tzatziki Sauce:

1. In a medium bowl combine the yogurt, olive oil, vinegar, lemon juice, garlic, dill and season to taste.
2. If grated, add in the cucumber, if spiralizing it leave it out.
3. Refrigerate covered until needed.

For the Salmon:

1. Preheat oven to 400 degrees F.
2. In a small bowl, combine the olive oil, lemon zest, garlic, and season to taste.
3. Lightly oil a large piece of foil that is twice the size of the salmon filets.
4. Place the salmon skin side down over the foil, brush with the garlic olive oil and fold the foil on top.
5. Place foil packet on a rimmed baking sheet.

6. Bake for 16 to 20 minutes or until cooked through.
7. Remove the salmon from the foil with a spatula - the skin will stick to the foil and the filets will come out in one piece.
8. Serve over the bed of cucumber noodles and top it with the tzatziki sauce.

Macros Per Serving – Calories: 439 |Total Fat: 26g |Protein: 41g |**Net Carbs: 4g**

Fish Tacos

You can still celebrate Taco Tuesday by whipping up a batch of crunchy and flaky keto-friendly fish tacos with this recipe!

Prep Time: 20 Minutes
Cook Time: 15 Minutes
Total Time: 2 Hours
Serves: 8

Ingredients:

- 8 oz. firm white-flesh fish such as flounder or cod
- 1/3 cup sour cream or coconut cream with 2 tsp. apple cider vinegar
- 2 tsp. apple cider vinegar
- 4 cloves garlic, pressed
- Kosher salt, to taste
- ½ cup whey protein isolate
- 1 tsp. baking powder
- 1 ½ tsp. chili powder
- ¼ - ½ tsp. kosher salt, to taste
- 1 egg
- 1 Tbsp. sour cream or coconut cream
- 2 tsp. apple cider vinegar
- Coconut oil or cooking oil, of choice

For Serving:
- 1 batch keto-friendly grain-free tortillas
- 1 batch pico de gallo salsa
- Guacamole
- Limes

Directions:

1. In a bowl, mix the sour or coconut cream, vinegar, garlic and season to taste with salt.
2. Prepare the fish by cutting the fish across the grain of the flesh into strips that are about ½ inch wide.
3. Add the fish to the cream marinade, cover and refrigerate for two hours or preferably overnight.
4. Place a skillet or pan over medium/low heat, add the oil about ½-inch deep.
5. While the oil heats up, mix together the whey protein, baking powder, chili powder and salt in a shallow plate or dish, set aside.

66

6. In a different place or dish whisk together the egg, cream and vinegar, set aside.
7. Prepare the fish by lightly removing excess marinade, dip it in the egg mix, followed by the whey protein mix.
8. Immediately placing it the hot oil and basting the top, frying it on both sides until deep golden and then transfer to a paper-lined plate for a couple minutes.
9. Serve right away with the heated tortillas, plenty of limes and your salsa of choice!

Recipe Notes:

- You can also make your own chili powder mix with ¾ tsp. paprika, ¼ tsp. garlic powder, ¼ tsp. onion powder, ¼ tsp. dried oregano, 1/8 tsp. cayenne pepper and 1/8 tsp. dried cumin.

Macros Per Serving (1 Fish Taco)– Calories: 48 |Protein: 9g |**Net Carbs: 2g (from the keto-friendly tortilla)**

Maple Walnut Crusted Salmon

Deliciously made with a sweet maple pecan crust, this flaky salmon is the perfect meal for dinner!

Prep Time: 5 Minutes 2-3 Hours
Cook Time: 10 Minutes
Total Time: 15 Minutes, 2-3 Hours
Serves: 4

Ingredients:
- 2 Tbsp. ghee, for pan
- 6 oz. salmon fillets
- A pinch of salt
- A pinch of pepper

Maple Walnut Crust:
- ½ cup finely chopped walnuts
- 1 tsp. smoked paprika
- ½ tsp. chipotle powder
- ½ tsp. onion powder
- ½ tsp. cracked black pepper
- 3 Tbsp. Sukrin gold fiber syrup or alternative syrup
- 1 Tbsp. apple cider vinegar
- 1 tsp. coconut aminos

Directions:
1. Prepare the maple walnut crust by combining the finely chopped walnuts, smoked paprika, chipotle powder, onion powder, black pepper, Sukrin gold fiber syrup, apple cider vinegar and coconut aminos in a small bowl, stir well to combine.
2. Place the salmon fillets on a plate and spoon the walnut mixture over each piece of fish, distributing it evenly.
3. Place in the refrigerator, uncovered, for 2 to 3 hours.
4. Preheat the oven to 425 degrees F.
5. In a large oven-safe skillet over high heat, add the ghee.
6. Once heated, add the pieces of fish and allow them to cook undisturbed for about 2 minutes, allowing the skin to sear.
7. Transfer the salmon from the pan to the oven and continue cooking the fish for about 5-8 minutes, depending on desired doneness and thickness of the fillets.
8. Drizzle the salmon with some of the melted ghee and additional syrup for serving, if desired.

Macros Per Serving – Calories: 443 |Total Fat: 27.3g |Protein: 40.2g |**Net Carbs: 10.9g**

Salmon Stuffed Avocado

Revamp a basic, everyday avocado into something incredibly tasty with this amazing Salmon Stuffed Avocado recipe!

Prep Time: 10 Minutes
Cook Time: 20 Minutes
Total Time: 30 Minutes
Serves: 6

Ingredients:

- 2 small medium or 1 large avocado, seed removed
- 2 small salmon fillets – 6.2 oz. cooked
- 1 small white onion, finely chopped
- ¼ cup sour cream or crème fraîche or mayonnaise
- 2 Tbsp. fresh lemon juice
- 1 Tbsp. ghee or coconut oil
- 1-2 Tbsp. dill, freshly chopped
- Salt, to taste
- Freshly ground black pepper, to taste

Garnish:

- Lemon wedges

Directions:

1. Place the salmon filets on a baking tray lined with parchment paper.
2. Drizzle with melted ghee or olive oil, then season with salt and pepper and 1 Tbsp. of fresh lemon juice.
3. Place in the oven and bake for 20 to 25 minutes.
4. Once done, remove from the oven and allow it to cool down for 5-10 minutes.
5. Using a fork, shred the salmon fillets and discard of the skin.
6. In a bowl, add the shredded salmon with the finely chopped onion, sour cream and freshly chopped dill, a squeeze of lemon juice and season with salt and pepper to taste.
7. Scoop out the middle of the avocado, leaving ½ to 1 inch of avocado.
8. Cut the scooped-out avocado into smaller pieces and place it into the bowl with the salmon, mix well to combine.
9. Fill each avocado half with the salmon and avocado mixture, add lemon.
10. Enjoy!

Macros Per Serving – Calories: 463 |Total Fat: 34.6g |Protein: 27g |**Net Carbs: 6.4g**

Zucchini Noodles with Garlic Shrimp

Just toss together Zucchini noodles with garlic shrimp and you'll have a delicious, healthy meal in just 20 minutes!

Prep Time: 15 Minutes
Cook Time: 6 Minutes
Total Time: 21 Minutes
Serves: 4

Ingredients:
- 6 zucchini, washed
- 1 lb. shrimp, peeled and deveined
- 2 cloves garlic, minced
- 1 tsp. paprika
- ½ tsp. chili flakes
- Juice of 1 lemon
- 2 Tbsp. olive oil
- ½ tsp. salt
- ¼ tsp. pepper
- 2 Tbsp. fresh parsley, finely chopped

Directions:
1. Create the zucchini noodles by using a spiral slicer to cut the zucchini into noodles and then place them into a colander over a bowl or in the sink.
2. Sprinkle the zucchini with salt and toss to combine.
3. Allow the zucchini to sit for 15 minutes while the salt extracts the excess moisture.
4. In the meantime, combine the garlic, paprika, chili flakes, lemon juice and shrimp in a bowl, mix well.
5. In a large skillet over medium high heat, add the olive oil.
6. Once heated, add the shrimp and season with salt and pepper.
7. Sauté until the shrimp is done, about 5 to 8 minutes.
8. Rinse the zucchini under running water to remove the salt and dry on paper towels.
9. Add the zucchini noodles and parsley to the garlic shrimp, toss to coat and serve.
10. Enjoy!

Macros Per Serving – Calories: 231 |Total Fat: 9.7g |Protein: 26.8g |**Net Carbs: 8.4g**

Finis Seared Tuna Salad with Wasabi Butter

This panko-and-sesame crusted seared tuna on a bed of arugula and spinach, all topped with a wasabi butter sauce, takes Japanese food to whole new level!

Prep Time: 5 Minutes
Cook Time: 10 Minutes
Total Time: 15 Minutes
Serves: 2-4

Ingredients:

- 3 Tbsp. black and white sesame seed
- 4 (5 oz.) raw ahi or yellowfin tuna steaks (I used Trader Joes frozen ahi tuna steaks)
- ½ tsp. kosher salt
- Freshly ground black pepper, to taste
- Canola oil or cooking spray
- 2 Tbsp. reduced sodium or gluten-free soy sauce
- 1 tsp. prepared wasabi paste
- 2 tsp. shallots, minced
- ¼ cup white wine
- 2 Tbsp. whole milk
- 2 Tbsp. unsalted butter
- 4 cups fresh baby arugula
- 4 cups fresh baby spinach

Optional:

- Sliced radish, for garnish
- Sliced cucumber, for garnish

Directions:

1. Place sesame seeds on a large plate or shallow bowl.
2. Season the tuna with salt and pepper, to taste.
3. Gently press both sides of each tuna steak with the sesame seeds.
4. In a large skillet over medium-high heat, add the oil or spray with oil.
5. Add 2 tuna steaks, spray each with oil and then allow them to cook 2 to 3 minutes, or until the outer edge becomes opaque. Flip each steak, spray with oil and cook for an additional 2 minutes, or until the outer edge are also opaque, the repeat this step with remaining 2 steaks.
6. Once cooked, set the steaks on a cutting board to rest and cool.
7. In the meantime, combine the soy sauce and wasabi paste in a small bowl, set aside.

8. In a small skillet over medium-low heat, add shallots and wine, simmer until reduced by half, 2-3 minutes. Add the milk and whisk constantly until the sauce no longer looks separated and has slightly thickened (about 1 minute).

9. Remove from heat and whisk in soy and wasabi paste mixture. Add butter and whisk to combine.

10. To serve: Distribute arugula and spinach evenly among 4 shallow bowls. Thinly slice the tuna and top each bed of lettuce with 1 tuna steak. Drizzle each with about 1 ½ Tbsp. of sauce. Serve.

Macros Per Serving – Calories: 311 |Total Fat: 11g |Protein: 37g |**Net Carbs: 9.5g**

Easy Shrimp Scampi

Make the quickest Shrimp Scampi ever with this super easy foil packet recipe that's perfect on a busy night!

Prep Time: 10 Minutes
Cook Time: 10 Minutes
Total Time: 20 Minutes
Serves: 4

Ingredients:

- 40 jumbo shrimp, peeled and deveined, about 1 lb.
- 2 Tbsp. unsalted butter, melted
- 4 garlic cloves, 2 grated, 2 thinly sliced
- ½ tsp. kosher salt
- 1 Tbsp. extra virgin olive oil
- ¼ cup dry white wine
- 1 Tbsp. fresh lemon juice
- 4 pinches red pepper flakes
- 3 Tbsp. chopped parsley
- 1 lemon, cut into wedges
- Heavy-Duty Aluminum Foil

Directions:

1. In a medium bowl, whisk together the grated garlic, salt and oil.
2. Add in the shrimp, toss to coat, and chill, uncovered for at least 30 minutes or for 1 hour.
3. Make the foil packets by tearing off 4 16" sheets of aluminum foil.
4. Place 10 shrimp on the center of each foil sheet, then top each with the remaining garlic slices, 1 Tbsp. wine, lemon juice, a pinch of red pepper flakes and 1/2 Tbsp. melted butter over each.
5. Close the packets by bringing up the long sides of the foil, so the ends meet over the food, then double fold the ends, leaving enough room for heat to circulate inside. Then double fold the two short ends to seal the packet.
6. Grill over high heat, 8 minutes, using gloves or tongs to remove and carefully open it or bake the packets in the oven, preheat the oven to 425 degrees F for 10 minutes.
7. Top the shrimp with chopped parsley.
8. Serve with lemon wedges.

Macros Per Serving – Calories: 224 |Total Fat: 11g |Protein: 24g |**Net Carbs: 4.5g**

California Avocado Stuffed with Spicy Crab

Make a delicious lunch in just 10 minutes with this California Spicy Crab Stuffed Avocados recipe that is finished with furikake and coconut aminos!

Prep Time: 10 Minutes

Total Time: 10 Minutes

Serves: 2

Ingredients:

- 2 Tbsp. mayo
- 2 tsp. sriracha, plus more for drizzling
- 1 tsp. chopped fresh chives
- 4 oz. lump crab meat
- ¼ cup peeled and diced cucumber
- 1 small Hass avocado, about 4 oz. avocado when pitted and peeled
- ½ tsp. furikake or sesame seeds
- 2 tsp. coconut aminos

Directions:

1. In a medium bowl, combine the mayo, sriracha and chopped chives.
2. Add in the crab meat and cucumber, gently toss to combine, set aside.
3. Cut the avocado open, remove the pit and peel the skin or simply spoon the avocado out.
4. Fill the avocado halves equally with the crab salad.
5. Top with furikake or sesame seeds and drizzle with coconut aminos.
6. Enjoy!

Macros Per Serving (½ stuffed avocado) – Calories: 194 |Total Fat: 13g |Protein: 12g |**Net Carbs: 3g**

Cauliflower Rice with King Crab

Made with Asian inspired cauliflower rice with bits of king crab, this amazing fried rice recipe will soon be your favorite!

Prep Time: 10 Minutes
Cook Time: 20 Minutes
Total Time: 30 Minutes
Serves: 4

Ingredients:

- 1 lb. (2 frozen) King crab legs
- 24 oz. riced cauliflower
- 1 Tbsp. sesame oil
- 2 large eggs, beaten
- Pinch of salt
- ½ small onion, finely diced
- 2 garlic cloves, minced
- 5 scallions, diced, whites and greens separated
- 3 Tbsp. coconut aminos
- Cooking spray

Directions:

1. Prepare the cauliflower rice by placing a few florets at a time into the food processor and pulse until the cauliflower is small and resembles the texture of rice or couscous – make sure you don't over process or it will be mushy. Set aside the cauliflower rice and repeat with the remaining cauliflower florets in batches.
2. In a large pot, add about 2 inches of water and bring to a boil.
3. Add in the crab leg and cook, covered until heated through for about 10 minutes.
4. Once cooked, remove the crab from the shell and lightly flake, set aside.
5. Add the egg to a bowl and seasoning with a pinch of salt, set aside.
6. In a large skillet or wok over medium heat, spray with oil.
7. Once heated, add the eggs and cook, turning a few times until set, then set aside.
8. Reduce the heat to medium-low, add in the sesame oil and sauté the onions, scallion whites, and garlic for about 3 to 4 minutes, or until soft.
9. Raise the heat to medium-high.
10. Add in the cauliflower "rice" to the sauté pan along with coconut aminos.
11. Mix well, then cover and cook for approximately 5 to 6 minutes, stirring occasionally, until the cauliflower is slightly crispy on the outside and tender on the inside.
12. Add the egg and crab, remove from heat and mix in scallion greens.
13. Serve!

Macros Per Serving (1 ½ cups)– Calories: 237 |Total Fat: 8g |Protein: 29.5g |**Net Carbs: 8g**

Poultry and Meat

Herbed Chicken with Saluted Mushrooms

Serve up a delicious main dish of tender chicken with mushrooms in a creamy, savory herb sauce!

Prep Time: 10 Minutes
Cook Time: 35 Minutes
Total Time: 45 Minutes
Serves: 4

Ingredients:
- 8 skin-on chicken thighs
- 2 tsp. sea salt
- ½ tsp. black pepper
- 1 Tbsp. and 1 tsp. dried oregano
- 1 Tbsp. and 1 tsp. dried thyme
- 1 Tbsp. and 1 tsp. dried rosemary
- 2 Tbsp. olive oil
- 8 oz. cremini mushrooms, quartered
- 2 cloves garlic, minced
- 1 cup chicken stock
- 2 Tbsp. Dijon mustard

Optional:
- Torn fresh parsley, as garnish

Directions:
1. Preheat the oven to 400 degrees F.
2. Season the chicken thighs on both sides with salt, pepper, 2 tsp. of the oregano, 2 tsp. of the dried thyme, and 2 tsp. of the dried rosemary.
3. Place a large cast iron skillet over medium heat, add the olive oil.
4. Once heated, add the chicken to the skillet, skin side down, cook for 5 to 6 minutes until the skin is crispy.
5. Flip the chicken thighs over to the other side and then place the skillet to the oven.
6. Bake for 15 to 20 minutes, until the chicken is cooked through.
7. Once done, place the skillet back to the stovetop, then remove the chicken from the pan, set aside, and cover to keep warm.
8. In the same skillet over medium heat, add the mushrooms and cook for 5 minutes, until they release their liquids and are tender.

9. Then add the garlic, chicken stock, Dijon mustard, and the remaining seasonings and cook for an additional 3 minutes.
10. Transfer the chicken to a plate and pour the sauce over top.
11. Serve and garnish with fresh parsley.

Macros Per Serving – Calories: 418 |Total Fat: 29g | Protein: 53g| **Net Carbs: 2.5g**

Chicken Tetrazzini

Make an amazing low carb chicken tetrazzini on those nights where you're just craving pasta!

Prep Time: 40 Minutes
Cook Time: 1 Hour
Total Time: 1 Hour 40 Minutes
Serves: 2

Ingredients:

- 3 zucchini medium
- 2 Tbsp. butter
- ½ onion, diced
- 2 cups mushrooms, sliced
- 1 clove garlic, minced
- 2 chicken breasts boneless, skinless, chopped
- 1.5 cups heavy cream
- 1 tsp. xantham gum
- ¼ cup mozzarella cheese shredded
- Salt, to sweat zucchini noodles
- Salt, to taste

Directions:

1. Prepare the noodles by spiralizing each zucchini into spaghetti noodle shapes using a spiralizer tool. Then add salt to the zucchini noodles and layout them over a folded paper towels to remove excess moisture. Allow the zucchini noodles to sit for 30 minutes, then squeeze them to remove any additional water.
2. Preheat oven to 400 degrees F.
3. In a large saucepan over medium heat, melt the butter.
4. Once heated, add the onion, mushrooms, and garlic to the pan, stirring as needed.
5. Once the onions become translucent, add the chopped chicken breast and increase temperature to medium-high.
6. When the chicken cooks to white in color, add in the heavy cream and thoroughly mix, all while bringing the sauce to a boil.
7. Once the cream is broiling, reduce the heat and allow the sauce to simmer for an additional 1 to 2 minutes.
8. Remove the sauce from heat and whisk in the xantham gum little by little to thicken up - If you prefer a thinner, runnier sauce, leave it out or cut the amount in half.

9. Arrange zucchini noodles in the bottom of a deep casserole dish, cover the entire bottom of the bakeware about an inch thick. Use a 9 x 6-inch dish for 10 servings of this recipe.
10. Add the creamy chicken mushroom sauce on top of the zucchini noodles, smooth the mixture evenly over the top and distribute it throughout the casserole dish.
11. Sprinkle mozzarella cheese on top.
12. Bake for 40 minutes, until the top is brown.
13. Enjoy.

Recipe Notes:
- If you want to add more protein to this dish, add extra chicken breast to the recipe.

Macros Per Serving – Calories: 194 |Total Fat: 16g |Protein: 7g |**Net Carbs: 4g**

Cobb Salad

Packed with protein, this simple Cobb salad that's topped with bacon, chicken breast slices, tomato and avocado is perfect for lunch.

Prep Time: 10 Minutes
Cook Time: 5 Minutes
Total Time: 15 Minutes
Serves: 1-2

Ingredients:

- 2 strips bacon
- 2 oz. chicken breast
- ½ campari tomato
- ¼ avocado
- 1 cup spinach
- 1 hard-boiled egg
- ½ tsp. white vinegar
- 1 Tbsp. olive oil

Directions:

1. Shred or slice the cook chicken, whichever one you prefer, set aside.
2. Dice the tomato and avocado, set aside.
3. Slice the hard-boiled egg, set aside.
4. Place the spinach in a large mixing bowl.
5. Top with the diced tomatoes, hard-boiled egg, avocado, chicken breast and bacon strips.
6. Top with the oil and vinegar
7. Toss to combine and enjoy!

Macros Per Serving – Calories: 600 |Total Fat: 48g |Protein: 43g |**Net Carbs: 3g**

Chicken Enchilada Bowls

Covered in a flavorful and rich Mexican sauce, this chicken enchilada bowl recipe is simple enough to make in one pot (or skillet) in just 30 minutes!

Prep Time: 10 Minutes
Cook Time: 20 Minutes
Total Time: 30 Minutes
Serves: 4

Ingredients:

- 2-3 chicken breasts, about 1 lb. of chicken, cut into 3 to 4 pieces
- ¾ cups red enchilada sauce
- ¼ cup water
- ¼ cup onion
- 1 (4 oz. can) green chiles
- 1 (12 oz.) steam bag cauliflower rice
- Salt, to taste

Toppings:

- Avocado
- Jalapeño
- Cheese
- Roma tomatoes

Directions:

1. In skillet over medium heat, add the chicken and cook the chicken breasts 10-15 minutes, until lightly brown.
2. Then add in the enchilada sauce, chiles, onions, water and reduce the heat to simmer.
3. Cover and cook until chicken is done.
4. Once the chicken is cooked, transfer the chicken to a plate and shred it with two forks.
5. Place the chicken back into sauce and continue simmering for another 10 minutes uncovered or until most of the liquid has been soaked up.
6. Prepare cauliflower rice as per instructions.
7. Top the cauliflower rice with enchilada chicken, cheese, avocado and tomatoes.

Macros Per Serving – Calories: 120 |Total Fat: 2g |Protein: 18g |**Net Carbs: 5g**
*Toppings have not been included in these nutritional totals.

Chicken Taco Lettuce Wraps

Spice up Taco Night with these low-carb lettuce wraps filled with taco-spiced chicken, creamy avocado, tomato, and drizzled with a homemade zesty cilantro lime sauce.

Prep Time: 15 Minutes
Cook Time: 15 Minutes
Total Time: 30 Minutes
Serves: 4

Ingredients:

Grilled Taco Chicken:

- 1 lb. Boneless, skinless chicken breasts or thighs
- 2 Tbsp. taco seasoning
- 2 cloves garlic, minced
- 1 Tbsp. olive oil

To Assemble:

- 8 leaves Romaine Lettuce rinsed
- 1 avocado diced
- 1 tomato diced
- ¼ cup onion diced

Cilantro Sauce:

- ½ cup loosely packed cilantro
- ¼ cup Greek Yogurt or sour-cream or mayo
- 2 Tbsp. olive oil
- 1 jalapeño optional
- 1 clove garlic minced
- Juice of 1 lime
- Pinch of salt

Directions:

1. In a large bowl or zip-seal bag, add in the chicken, garlic, olive oil, and spices.
2. Place in fridge and allow it to marinate for at least 15-30 minutes or up to 24 hours.
3. Remove the chicken from marinade and discard marinade.
4. Place the chicken on a grill or in a pan heated to medium-high heat, and cook the chicken until it's no longer pink on the inside, about 9-10 minutes per side.
5. Once done, allow the chicken to rest.
6. Prepare the cilantro sauce by combining the cilantro, Greek yogurt or sour cream or mayo, olive oil, optional jalapeno, minced garlic, lime juice and a pinch of salt in a food processor and blend for 1 minute or until creamy.
7. Assemble by layering a lettuce wraps with chicken, tomatoes, onion, and avocado.

8. Drizzle with cilantro sauce or your favorite taco sauce.
9. Serve!

Macros Per Serving (1 Taco) – Calories: 161 |Total Fat: 9.1g |Protein: 14.5g |**Net Carbs: 4.9g**

Roasted Lemon Chicken

Coated in a butter and herb sauce, this roasted lemon chicken recipe is easy to make and pairs well with your favorite veggies.

Prep Time: 5 Minutes
Cook Time: 35 Minutes
Total Time: 40 Minutes
Serves: 4

Ingredients:

- 1 ¼ lbs. boneless skinless chicken breasts
- 1 Tbsp. olive oil
- 1 tsp. Italian seasoning
- 3 Tbsp. butter, melted
- 1 tsp. minced garlic
- ¼ cup chicken broth
- 2 Tbsp. lemon juice
- 1 Tbsp. chopped parsley
- Salt, to taste
- Pepper, to taste

Optional:

- Lemon slices, for serving

Directions:

1. Preheat the oven to 400 degrees F.
2. Season the chicken breasts on both sides with salt, pepper and the Italian seasoning.
3. In a large pan over medium high heat, add the olive oil.
4. Once heated, add the chicken breasts and cook for 3 to 5 minutes on each side or until browned, then transfer the chicken to a baking dish.
5. In a small bowl, mix together the butter, garlic, chicken broth and lemon juice, pour the butter mixture over the chicken.
6. Bake for 25 minutes or until chicken is cooked through, true bake time will depend on the thickness of the chicken breasts.
7. Spoon the sauce on the bottom of the baking dish over the chicken, then sprinkle with parsley.
8. Serve and garnish with lemon slices.

Recipe Notes:

- If your chicken breasts are less than 1 inch thick, then decrease the bake time accordingly.

Macros Per Serving – Calories: 271 |Total Fat: 15g |Protein: 30g |**Net Carbs: 0g**

Cheddar Chicken and Broccoli Casserole

Broccoli and cheddar together make an amazing combination! So, why not make this delicious, low carb Cheddar Chicken and Broccoli Casserole for dinner any night of the week.

Prep Time: 10 Minutes
Cook Time: 25 Minutes
Total Time: 35 Minutes
Serves: 4

Ingredients:

- 20 oz. chicken breast, cooked and shredded
- 2 Tbsp. olive oil
- 2 cups broccoli, frozen or fresh (steamed or broiled)
- ½ cup sour cream
- ½ cup heavy cream
- 1 cup cheddar cheese
- 1 oz. pork rinds
- ½ tsp. paprika
- 1 tsp. oregano
- Salt, to taste
- Pepper, to taste

Directions:

1. Preheat oven to 450 degrees F.
2. In a deep mixing bowl, combine the shredded chicken, frozen broccoli florets or steamed broccoli florets, olive oil and sour cream, mix thoroughly to combine.
3. Place the chicken and broccoli into a greased 8x11 inch baking dish, spread them into an even layer, pressing firmly - the casserole should be slightly packed.
4. Drizzle heavy cream over the top layer of the casserole.
5. Then add the salt, pepper, paprika and oregano.
6. Add a cup of shredded cheddar cheese to the top of your casserole all the way up to the edges.
7. In a ziploc bag, add 1 oz. of pork rinds and crush them with your hands or a rolling pin.
8. Add these crushed pork rinds over the shredded cheese as a crispy casserole topping.

9. Bake for about 20 to 25 minutes, until the entire casserole is bubbling slightly and the edges brown.
10. Serve with a side of marinara sauce.
11. Enjoy!

Macros Per Serving – Calories: 365 |Total Fat: 28g |Protein: 29g |**Net Carbs: 2.6g**

Hearty Chicken Soup

Comforting and healthy, this low carb chicken soup is loaded with protein and veggies that are so good for you!

Prep Time: 10 Minutes
Cook Time: 35 Minutes
Total Time: 45 Minutes
Serves: 8

Ingredients:

- 10 cups bone broth or chicken stock
- ½ tsp. garlic powder
- ½ tsp. dried oregano
- 1 cup thinly sliced celery
- ¼ cup chopped fresh parsley
- 1 Tbsp. apple cider vinegar
- 4 cups cooked, shredded or chopped chicken
- 1 ½ cups diced butternut squash
- 2 cups jicama, peeled and chopped small rice like pieces
- Sea salt, to taste
- Pepper, to taste

Directions:

1. In a large pot, combine the broth, garlic powder, dried oregano, celery, butternut squash and jicama.
2. Bring to a boil, then lower heat and simmer uncovered for 30 minutes, or until veggies are fork tender.
3. Add the chicken and cook for another 5 minutes, or until heated through - making sure not to overcook the chicken.
4. Remove from the heat.
5. Add the parsley and apple cider vinegar.
6. Season with sea salt and pepper to taste.
7. Serve!

Macros Per Serving – Calories: 190 |Total Fat: 5g |Protein: 26g |**Net Carbs: 4g**

Creamy Garlic Chicken Soup

Creamy with a touch of garlic, this warm and comforting soup is all you need for dinner on a cold night!

Prep Time: 10 Minutes
Cook Time: 10 Minutes
Total Time: 20 Minutes
Serves: 2

Ingredients:

- 1 Tbsp. butter
- 2 cups shredded chicken, about 1 large chicken breast
- 4 oz. cream cheese cubed
- 2 Tbsp. garlic seasoning
- 14.5 oz. chicken broth
- ¼ cup heavy cream
- Salt, to taste

Directions:

1. In a saucepan over medium heat, melt butter.
2. Once heated, add in the shredded chicken to pan and coat with melted butter.
3. As chicken heats up, add in the cubes of cream cheese and garlic gusto seasoning. mix well to combine.
4. Once the cream cheese is melted and evenly distributed, add in the chicken broth and heavy cream.
5. Bring to a boil, then reduce heat to low and simmer for 3 to 4 minutes.
6. Season with the salt to taste.
7. Serve!

Recipe Notes:

- Create the garlic gusto seasoning by combing a mix of parsley, garlic, onion, lemon peel and paprika.

Macros Per Serving – Calories: 307 |Total Fat: 25g |Protein: 2.5g |**Net Carbs: 18.5g**

Shredded Chicken Chili

Enjoy this Shredded Chicken Chili on those busy days when you need a filling keto-friendly meal in a hurry!

Prep Time: 5 Minutes
Cook Time: 25 Minutes
Total Time: 30 Minutes
Serves: 4

Ingredients:

- 4 chicken breasts large, shredded
- 1 Tbsp. butter
- ½ onion chopped
- 2 cups chicken broth
- 10 oz. diced tomatoes canned, undrained
- 2 oz. tomato paste
- 1 Tbsp. chili powder
- 1 Tbsp. cumin
- ½ Tbsp. garlic powder
- 4 oz. cream cheese
- Salt, to taste
- Pepper to taste

Optional:

- 1 jalapeño pepper, chopped
- Monterey jack cheese, toppings
- Cilantro, toppings

Directions:

1. Prepare the chicken by boiling chicken breasts in water or broth on stovetop that covers the breasts for 10 to 12 minutes. Once the meat is no longer pink, remove from the pot and shred with two forks.
2. In a large stockpot over medium-high heat, melt the butter.
3. Once heated, add the onion and cook until translucent.
4. Add in the shredded chicken, chicken broth, diced tomatoes, tomato paste, chili powder, cumin, garlic powder, and jalapeño to the pot, stir gently to combine.
5. Bring to a boil, then turn the heat down to a simmer over medium-low heat and cover for 10 minutes.
6. Cut the cream cheese into small, 1-inch chunks.
7. Remove the lid and mix in the cream cheese, increase the heat back up to medium-high and continue to stir until the cream cheese is completely blended in.

8. Remove chili from heat and season with salt and pepper to taste.
9. Enjoy!

Macros Per Serving – Calories: 201 |Total Fat: 11g |Protein: 18g |**Net Carbs: 6g**

Chipotle Steak Bowl

This low carb beef stew is so rich in flavor and includes tender beef chucks and perfectly cooked vegetables.

Prep Time: 15 Minutes
Cook Time: 8 Minutes
Total Time: 23 Minutes
Serves: 4

Ingredients:

- 16 oz. skirt steak
- Salt, to taste
- Pepper, to taste
- 4 oz. pepper jack cheese
- 1 cup sour cream
- 1 handful fresh cilantro
- 1 splash Chipotle Tabasco Sauce
- 1 -2 cups of guacamole (homemade or store-brought)

Directions:

1. Prepare the skirt steak by seasoning it with a sprinkle of salt and pepper.
2. Place a cast iron skillet on high heat, once it's hot, cook the skirt steak for 3-4 minutes on each side.
3. Transfer the steak to rest on a plate for about 5 minutes.
4. Slice the skirt steak against the grain into thin, bite-sized strips and divide into 4 portions, season to taste.
5. Shred the pepper jack cheese using a cheese grater and top on each portion of skirt steak.
6. Add about 1/4 cup of guacamole to each portion.
7. Then add 1/4 cup of sour cream.
8. Top with the optional Chipotle Tabasco Sauce and fresh cilantro.
9. Enjoy!

Macros Per Serving – Calories: 620 |Total Fat: 50g |Protein: 33g |**Net Carbs: 5.5g**

Philly Cheesesteak Stuffed Peppers

Complete with roast beef, onions, and tender mushrooms, these easy to make Philly cheesesteak stuffed peppers make lunch-time 100% better!

Prep Time: 10 Minutes
Cook Time: 30 Minutes
Total Time: 40 Minutes
Serves: 2

Ingredients:
- 3 bell peppers, cut in half lengthwise, ribs and seeds removed
- 2 Tbsp. butter or bacon fat, divided
- 1 medium to large yellow onion, julienned
- 8 oz. crimini mushrooms, sliced
- 2 lbs. roast beef sandwich cuts into strips or 4 boxes (9 oz. each) beef steaks
- 4 cloves garlic, minced
- 1 tsp. mineral salt
- ½ tsp. cayenne pepper
- ¾ cup mozzarella, provolone, or pepper jack cheese, shredded, divided

Optional:
- ¼ tsp. red pepper flakes

Directions:
1. Preheat the oven to 400 degree F.
2. Grease a 9- by 13-inch dish.
3. Then place the pepper halves in the dish and pre-bake for about 10 to 15 minutes, until soft.
4. In the meanwhile, place skillet over medium-high heat and melt 1 tablespoon butter.
5. Once heated, add the onions and mushrooms and sauté, stirring often, until the onions are translucent.
6. Add the remaining butter, roast beef, garlic, salt, cayenne pepper, and red pepper flakes to the skillet Sauté for an additional 10 to 15 minutes, or until the onions are caramelized and meat is heated.
7. Remove the peppers from the oven, add about 1 Tbsp. of cheese to the bottom of each pepper half.
8. Stuff the peppers with the meat mixture, top with remaining cheese.
9. Bake for 10 to 15 minutes, or until cheese is melted and they begin to lightly brown.
10. Enjoy!

Macros Per Serving – Calories: 302 |Total Fat: 13g |Protein: 37g |**Net Carbs: 5g**

Zucchini Beef Sauté with Garlic and Cilantro

Loaded with mushrooms, bell peppers and zucchini, this quick beef stir-fry is healthy and full of flavor!

Prep Time: 5 Minutes
Cook Time: 10 Minutes
Total Time: 15 Minutes
Serves: 2

Ingredients:

- 10 oz. beef, sliced into 1-2 inch strips against the grain
- 1 zucchini, cut into 1-2 inch, long thin strips
- ¼ cup cilantro, chopped
- 3 cloves of garlic, diced or minced
- 2 Tbsp. gluten-free tamari sauce or coconut aminos
- Avocado oil, coconut oil or olive oil for cooking

Directions:

1. Into a frying pan on high heat, add 2 Tbsp. of avocado.
2. Once heated, add the strips of beef into the frying pan, sauté for a few minutes on high heat.
3. Once the beef is browned, add in the zucchini strips and continue to sauté.
4. When the zucchini is soft, add in the tamari sauce, garlic, and cilantro, sauté for a few more minutes.
5. Serve!

Macros Per Serving – Calories: 500 |Total Fat: 40g |Protein: 31g |**Net Carbs: 4g**

Cream of Mushroom Pork Chops

Made all in one skillet, this recipe features flavorful pan seared pork chops covered in cream of mushroom.

Prep Time: 10 Minutes
Cook Time: 20 Minutes
Total Time: 30 Minutes
Serves: 4

Ingredients:
- 4 thin, bone-in pork chops (½ inch each)
- 2 ½ Tbsp. avocado oil, olive oil or bacon grease, divided
- 1 lb. sliced mushrooms
- 1 Tbsp. onion, minced
- 1 clove garlic, minced
- 1/3 cup dry white wine
- 1/3 cup unsalted chicken broth
- ½ cup heavy cream
- 1/8 tsp. powdered dried sage
- ¼ tsp. fresh thyme leaves, chopped
- Salt, to taste
- Pepper, to taste

Directions:
1. Allow the pork to reach room temperature, then rub both sides of the pork with about 2 tsp. of oil and season with salt and pepper.
2. Place a large pan over medium high heat, add 2 to 3 tsp. of oil to coat the bottom of the pan.
3. Once heated, add the pork chops to the pan and turn the heat down to medium, cook for about 3 1/3 minutes per side - If your pork chops are thicker or cold, add more cooking time.
4. Transfer to a plate and cover with a tent of foil.
5. Add 1 Tbsp. of oil to the pan and swirl to coat the pan.
6. Once heated, add the mushrooms and stir to coat, cook for 2 minutes, then stir the mushrooms.
7. Add in the onions and garlic, cook for 1 minute and stir, cook for an additional minute.
8. Add the wine and chicken broth scraping all of the brown bits off the bottom of the pan, allow it to simmer and reduce by half.

9. Then add in the heavy cream, powdered sage and fresh thyme, cook until the sauce thickens.
10. Season with salt and pepper to taste.
11. Pour the sauce over the pork chops and serve with cauliflower mash and green beans.

Macros Per Serving – Calories: 483 |Total Fat: 40g |Protein: 21g |**Net Carbs: 5g**

Egg Roll in a Bowl

Enjoy all the flavors of an egg roll in an easy to make bowl you can have for lunch or dinner in just 20 minutes!

Prep Time: 5 Minutes
Cook Time: 15 Minutes
Total Time: 20 Minutes
Serves: 4

Ingredients:

- 1 lb. ground pork
- 1 head cabbage thinly sliced
- ½ onion medium, thinly sliced
- 1 Tbsp. sesame oil
- ¼ cup soy sauce or liquid aminos
- 1 clove garlic, minced
- 1 tsp. ground ginger
- 2 Tbsp. chicken broth
- Salt, to taste
- Pepper, to taste
- 2 stalks of green onion

Directions:

1. In a large pan over medium heat, brown the ground pork.
2. Add in the sesame oil and onion to browned ground pork, mix together and continue to cook over medium heat.
3. In the meantime, mix together the soy sauce, garlic, and ground ginger in a small bowl.
4. Once the onions have browned, add the soy sauce mixture to the pan.
5. Then follow with the cabbage mixture to the pan and toss to evenly coat the vegetables.
6. Add in the chicken broth and mix.
7. Continue to cook over medium heat for 3 minutes, stirring frequently.
8. Garnish with salt, pepper, and green onion.
9. Serve!

Macros Per Serving – Calories: 268 |Total Fat: 18g |Protein: 15g |**Net Carbs: 6g**

Italian Sausage with Peppers and Onions in Marinara Sauce

Great on sandwiches or as is, this recipe features sweet Italian sausage cooked with colorful bell peppers and onions covered in a marinara sauce.

Prep Time: 10 Minutes
Cook Time: 20 Minutes
Total Time: 30 Minutes
Serves: 4

Ingredients:

- 1 lb. Italian sausage links
- 9 oz. mixed color bell pepper, sliced into strips (about 2 large peppers)
- 2 oz. sliced onion (about ½ cup)
- 1 Tbsp. olive oil (or more to taste)
- 1 tsp. minced garlic
- ½ cup Rao's Marinara Sauce
- Salt, to taste
- Pepper, to taste

Directions:

1. In a large skillet over medium heat, add the 1 ½ tsp. oil.
2. Once heated, add the sausage slices and brown for about 8-10 minutes.
3. Transfer the sausage to a plate.
4. In a clean pan, heat the 1 tsp. of oil over medium heat.
5. Once hot, sauté the bell peppers and onion with the minced garlic until softened about 10 minutes.
6. Add the sausage and any juices back to the pan to re-heat.
7. Add the Marinara sauce, stir to coat.
8. Taste and season with salt and pepper.
9. Serve!

Macros Per Serving – Calories: 420 |Total Fat: 32.5g |Protein: 23.5g |**Net Carbs: 6.5g**

Pork Chops Smothered in Caramelized Onion & Bacon

In just 55 minutes you can enjoy a juicy, tender pork chops smothered in a creamy onion and bacon sauce!

Prep Time: 10 Minutes
Cook Time: 45 Minutes
Total Time: 55 Minutes
Serves: 4

Ingredients:

- 6 slices bacon chopped
- 2 small onions thinly sliced
- ¼ tsp. salt
- ¼ pepper
- 4 bone-in pork chops 1 inch thick
- Salt, to taste
- Pepper to taste
- ½ cup chicken broth
- ¼ cup heavy cream

Directions:

1. In a large sauté pan over medium heat, cook bacon until crispy.
2. Once cooked, use a slotted spoon to transfer to a bowl, reserve the bacon grease.
3. Add the onions to bacon grease, season with salt and pepper, cook, stirring frequently for 10 minutes, until onions are soft and golden brown, then place the onions in the bowl with the bacon.
4. Increase the heat to medium high and season the pork chops with salt and pepper.
5. Add the chops to pan and brown on one side for 3 minutes, then turn the chops over and reduce the heat to medium, cooking on the other side until internal temperature reaches 135 degrees F, for about 7 to 10 more minutes.
6. Transfer the pork chops to a plate and tent with foil.
7. Add the broth to pan and scrape up the browned bits.
8. Add the cream and simmer until mixture is thickened, for about 2 to 3 minutes Return the onions and bacon back to the pan, stir to combine.
9. Top the pork chops with onion and bacon sauce.
10. Serve!

Macros Per Serving – Calories: 342 |Total Fat: 18g |Protein: 37g |**Net Carbs: 5.28g**

Classic Italian Meatballs

Make classic Italian meatballs that are juicy, tender and completely low carb with this recipe!

Prep Time: 15 Minutes
Cook Time: 20 Minutes
Total Time: 35 Minutes
Serves: 4-5

Ingredients:

- ½ lb. ground beef chuck, 85 % lean
- ½ lb. ground pork, turkey or veal
- ¼ cup Parmesan cheese, grated
- ¼ cup heavy cream
- 1 large egg, beaten
- 2 Tbsp. fresh parsley, minced
- 1 Tbsp. onion, finely grated
- 1 clove garlic, grated
- ½ tsp. salt
- ¼ tsp. pepper

Optional Sauce:

- 2 cups your favorite low carb marinara sauce

Directions:

1. In a medium bowl, add the beef and pork, and break up into smaller chunks, aiming to create an even mix.
2. Add parmesan cheese, heavy cream, beaten egg, parsley, finely grated onion, garlic, salt and pepper to the meat and mix with a hand mixer until combined - don't over-mix.
3. Lightly oil your hands and roll the meat into 12 meatballs, set aside.
4. Place a large frying pan over medium heat, add 1-2 tsp. of oil and swirl it to coat the pan.
5. Once hot, add the meatballs to the pan, making sure they don't touch or overcrowd it.
6. Cook the meatballs for approximately 1 ½ minutes per side, turning at least 4 times.
7. Cook for 10 to 15 minutes, until brown and then transfer the meatballs to a plate.
8. Heat the sauce in the same pan, scraping up the brown bits for a flavorful sauce or warm the sauce on the stove and pour over the meatballs.
9. Garnish with parsley.
10. Serve or top with mozzarella cheese and melt it under the broiler

Macros Per Serving – Calories: 387 |Total Fat: 22g |Protein: 19g |**Net Carbs: 1g**

Asian Sesame Beef Salad

You'll love serving up this delicious, crunchy salad that's topped with yummy sesame beef and tender mushrooms!

Prep Time: 5 Minutes
Cook Time: 15 Minutes
Total Time: 20 Minutes
Serves: 2

Ingredients:

For the salad:

- 20 oz. filet steak or any cut of your choice
- 6 oz. Enoki mushrooms or any mushroom of your choice
- 6 oz. mixed lettuce
- 1 tsp. sesame seeds not in the macros
- 1 Tbsp. butter
- 1 Tbsp. olive oil for frying
- Coriander to garnish
- ½ Tbsp. curry powder
- Salt, to taste

For the peanut soya dressing:

- 2 Tbsp. olive oil
- 1 Tbsp. peanut butter
- 1 clove garlic minced
- 1 tsp. soya sauce, one with the least carbs
- 1 tsp. white vinegar
- 1 dash fish sauce
- 1 squeeze lime juice
- 2 drops stevia
- Salt, to taste
- Pepper, to taste

Directions:

1. Prepare the dressing by mixing together the olive oil, peanut butter, minced garlic, soya sauce, white vinegar, fish sauce, lime juice, whisk to emulsify.
2. Cut and rinse the mushrooms, set aside.
3. Slice the beef into thin strips and season with the salt and curry powder.
4. Place a pan over medium-high heat, and fry the beef in batches, set aside.

5. In the same pan add some butter and stir fry the mushrooms, then season with salt while cooking.
6. Add in the resting juices from the beef into the pan and cook down till the liquid dries out.
7. Assemble the salad with the lettuce, seared beef, mushrooms and the dressing.
8. Finish with the coriander and sesame seeds.
9. Enjoy!

Veggies

Moroccan Roasted Green Beans

Change the way you think about boring green beans with these delicious Moroccan Spiced Roasted Green Beans!

Prep Time: 10 Minutes
Cook Time: 30 Minutes
Total Time: 40 Minutes
Serves: 6

Ingredients:

- 6 cups raw green beans, trimmed
- 1 tsp. kosher salt
- ½ tsp. ground black pepper
- 1 Tbsp. Ras el Hanout seasoning or Moroccan spice mix
- 2 Tbsp. olive oil

Directions:

1. Preheat oven to 400 degrees F.
2. Toss the green beans in olive oil and seasoning with the black pepper, salt and ras el hanout or Moroccan spice mix.
3. Layer them on a large cookie sheet or roasting pan.
4. Roast for 20 minutes.
5. Once cooked, remove from the oven and stir.
6. Return to the oven and roast for an additional 10 minutes.
7. Remove and serve warm or chilled.

Recipe Notes:

- You can easily make your own Moroccan spice mix by combining 1 ½ tsp. coriander seeds.
- ¾ tsp. cumin seeds, ½ tsp. crushed red pepper flakes, 1 ¼ tsp. ground cinnamon, 1 tsp. paprika, ½ tsp. ground cardamom, ½ tsp. ground ginger and ½ tsp. ground turmeric.

Macros Per Serving – Calories: 73 |Total Fat: 5g |Protein: 2g |**Net Carbs: 4g**

Parmesan Roasted Cauliflower

A simple side like Parmesan Roasted Cauliflower will easy complete a chicken or beef dinner! Plus it's super easy to clean up.

Prep Time: 10 Minutes
Cook Time: 45 Minutes
Total Time: 55 Minutes
Serves: 2

Ingredients:

- 8 oz. cauliflower florets, sliced horizontally
- 2 Tbsp. melted butter
- 1 Tbsp. olive oil
- Pinch of salt
- 3 light dashes of ground black pepper
- ½ cup Parmesan cheese
- 1 tsp. chopped parsley leaves

Directions:

1. Preheat oven to 400 degrees F.
2. In a bowl, add the sliced cauliflower, melted butter and oil, toss well to combine.
3. Season the cauliflower with salt and black pepper.
4. Transfer the cauliflower to a baking sheet, in a single layer, roast until almost tender about 20 to 30 minutes.
5. Once done, remove from the oven and sprinkle the grated Parmesan and the chopped parsley.
6. Roast again until the cheese melts and slightly crusty, about 5 minutes
7. Serve!

Macros Per Serving – Calories: 229 |Total Fat: 18.9g |Protein: 11.3g |**Net Carbs: 4.2g**

Mexican Cauliflower Rice

Transform cauliflower into a flavorful Mexican inspired dish with this easy to make Cauliflower "Rice" recipe!

Prep Time: 5 Minutes
Cook Time: 5 Minutes
Total Time: 10 Minutes
Serves: 4

Ingredients:

- 4 cups cauliflower, crumbled
- 1 tsp. olive oil
- ½ medium onion, finely diced
- 2 medium plum tomatoes, small diced
- 1 jalapeño, seeds and membrane removed, minced
- 2 garlic cloves, minced
- 2 Tbsp. tomato paste
- ½ tsp. cumin
- ¼ smoked paprika
- ¼ tsp. cayenne pepper
- 1 tsp. kosher salt
- Freshly ground black pepper, to taste
- Chopped cilantro

Directions:

1. In a large skillet over medium-high heat, add the oil.
2. Once heated, add the onions, tomatoes and jalapeño, sauté until tender, about 2 to 3 minutes.
3. Add in the garlic and cauliflower, sauté until the cauliflower is somewhat tender, 2 minutes.
4. Add in the tomato paste, cumin, paprika, cayenne, salt and pepper.
5. Stir to evenly coat the vegetables with the tomato paste and spices, cook for 1 minute or until heated through.
6. Top with the chopped cilantro.
7. Serve!

Macros Per Serving – Calories: 58 |Total Fat: 1.5g |Protein: 3g |**Net Carbs: 6g**

Creamy Cauliflower Mash

Creamy and buttery cauliflower mash are a healthy and delicious substitute for mashed potato!

Prep Time: 10 Minutes
Cook Time: 10 Minutes
Total Time: 20 Minutes
Serves: 2

Ingredients:

- 1 medium cauliflower, about 1.4lb
- 3 oz. butter
- 1 tsp. salt
- ½ tsp. pepper

Directions:

1. Place a large pot of water over high heat to bring to a boil.
2. Cut the cauliflower into evenly sized florets.
3. Gently place the cauliflower florets into the boiling water, cook for 5-8 minutes, or until tender.
4. Drain the cauliflower completely of the water and then return it to the warm pot.
5. In the warm pot, add the butter, salt and pepper.
6. Blend the cauliflower with an immersion blender until there are no lumps.
7. Allow the mash to sit and rest for 3 minutes.
8. Blend for a second time and allow it to rest and blend again to make the cauliflower extra smooth and creamy.
9. Serve and enjoy!

Macros Per Serving – Calories: 151 |Total Fat: 14g |Protein: 2g |**Net Carbs: 3g**

Roasted Parmesan Green Beans

Roasted to perfection, these tender crisp green beans are topped with shredded Parmesan cheese and ready in just 20 minutes!

Prep Time: 10 Minutes
Cook Time: 10 Minutes
Total Time: 20 Minutes
Serves: 4

Ingredients:

- 12 oz. green beans, trimmed and dry
- 2 tsp. olive oil
- ¼ tsp. garlic powder
- 1 ½ Tbsp. shredded Parmesan
- Kosher salt, to taste
- Pepper to taste

Directions:

1. Preheat the oven to 425 degrees F.
2. Line a baking sheet with aluminum foil.
3. Spread the green beans out on the baking sheet and drizzle the oil over them.
4. Season with salt, pepper and garlic powder and toss well to evenly coat.
5. Spread out the green beans making sure that they lay flat on the pan.
6. Bake 10 minutes, then shake the pan to turn and bake 5 additional minutes.
7. Remove the pan from the oven.
8. Sprinkle with grated cheese and salt if needed.
9. Serve!

Macros Per Serving – Calories: 55 |Total Fat: 3g |Protein: 2.5g |**Net Carbs: 3.5g**

Cheesy Zucchini Gratin

Cheesy and really creamy, this super easy Zucchini Gratin will instantly become a staple in your house!

Prep Time: 10 Minutes
Cook Time: 45 Minutes
Total Time: 55 Minutes
Serves: 9

Ingredients:
- 4 cups sliced raw zucchini
- 1 small onion, peeled and sliced thin
- 1 ½ cups shredded pepper jack cheese
- 2 Tbsp. butter
- ½ tsp. garlic powder
- ½ cup heavy whipping cream
- Salt, to taste
- Pepper, to taste

Directions:
1. Preheat oven to 375 degrees F.
2. Grease a 9×9 or equivalent oven proof pan.
3. Overlap 1/3 of the zucchini and onion slices in the greased pan, season with salt and pepper and then sprinkle with 1/2 cup of shredded cheese.
4. Repeat two more times until there are at least three layers and you have used up all of the zucchini, onions, and shredded cheese.
5. In a microwave safe bowl, combine the garlic powder, butter, and heavy cream.
6. Heat for one minute or until the butter has melted, stir to mix.
7. Gently pour the butter and cream mixture over the zucchini layers.
8. Bake for about 45 minutes, or until the liquid has thickened and the top is golden brown.
9. Serve!

Recipe Notes:
- Depending on your zucchini, you may have to cook it longer in order to reduce the sauce. If you find that it is very watery after the 45 minutes, lower the oven temp to 350 degrees F and cook for another 10 minutes or so.

Macros Per Serving – Calories: 230 |Total Fat: 20g |Protein: 8g |**Net Carbs: 3g**

Rainbow Vegetable Noodles

Add a dose of color to your plate with these colorful roasted rainbow vegetable noodles!

Prep Time: 15 Minutes
Cook Time: 20 Minutes
Total Time: 35 Minutes
Serves: 6

Ingredients:

- 1 medium zucchini
- 1 medium summer squash
- 1 large carrot
- 1 small sweet potato
- 4 oz. red onion
- 6 oz. mixed bell peppers
- 3 large cloves garlic
- 4 Tbsp. bacon fat, or olive oil, butter or ghee
- Sea salt, to taste
- Black pepper, to taste

Directions:

1. Preheat oven to 400 degrees F.
2. Coat a baking sheet with the bacon fat or olive oil, butter, or ghee.
3. Using a spiral slicer, spiral the zucchini, squash, carrot and sweet potato into noodle-like ribbons.
4. Then use a mandolin, on the thinnest setting or a knife to slice the red onion, bell peppers, and garlic.
5. In a bowl, add the vegetables, sprinkle with salt and pepper, and toss to combine.
6. Spread the vegetable noodles in a thin layer across baking sheet.
7. Bake for 20 minutes, tossing after 10 minutes.
8. Serve as a side.

Macros Per Serving – Calories: 128 |Total Fat: 9g |Protein: 2g |**Net Carbs: 8g**

Sautéed Mushrooms in White Wine Sauce with Thyme

Compliment your main dish with a side of sautéed mushrooms in a butter and white wine sauce finished with fresh thyme!

Prep Time: 5 Minutes
Cook Time: 10 Minutes
Total Time: 15 Minutes
Serves: 6

Ingredients:

- 1 lb. mushrooms
- 2 Tbsp. butter or olive oil
- 1 tsp. fresh thyme, chopped
- 1 Tbsp. butter or ghee
- 2 Tbsp. dry white wine
- 1-2 tsp. red wine vinegar
- Salt, to taste
- Pepper, to taste

Directions:

1. Wash the mushrooms in a colander and then dry well on a paper towels.
2. Cut off the dried part of the stem end and then slice each mushroom into quarter sizes.
3. In a sauté pan over medium heat, add 2 Tbsp. of butter or olive oil, covering the pan.
4. Once heated, add the mushrooms, stirring to cover the mushrooms with the butter or oil.
5. Cook the mushrooms for 3 minutes and then stir, cook another 2-3 minutes.
6. Then turn the heat down and add the butter, wine and thyme, cook until thyme is fragrant.
7. Remove the mushrooms from a pan and add 1 to 2 tsp. of red wine vinegar.
8. Season with salt and pepper to taste.
9. Serve!

Macros Per Serving – Calories: 113 |Total Fat: 10g |Protein: 2g |**Net Carbs: 4g**

Snap Pea Salad

Sweet, savory and fresh, this low-carb snap pea salad makes a perfect side next to a roasted chicken or beef dish.

Prep Time: 5 Minutes
Cook Time: 10 Minutes
Total Time: 40 Minutes
Serves: 4

Ingredients:
- 8 oz. cauliflower, riced
- ¼ cup lemon juice
- ¼ cup olive oil
- 1 clove garlic crushed
- ½ tsp. coarse grain dijon mustard
- 1 tsp. granulated stevia/erythritol blend
- ¼ tsp. pepper
- ½ tsp. sea salt
- ½ cup sugar snap peas ends removed and each pod cut into three pieces
- ¼ cup chives
- ½ cup sliced almonds
- ¼ cup red onions minced

Directions:
1. Pour 1 to 2 inches of water in a pot fitted with a steamer, bring water to a simmer.
2. Place the riced cauliflower in the steamer basket and sprinkle lightly with sea salt, cover, and place over the simmering water in the bottom of the steamer.
3. Steam the riced cauliflower until tender, about 10-12 minutes.
4. Once cauliflower is tender, remove the top of the steamer from the simmering water and place it over a bowl, draining out any excess water. Allow it to cool, uncovered for about 10 minutes, then cover and place the steamer and the bowl in the refrigerator, chill for at least 1/2 hour or until it's cool to the touch.
5. While the cauliflower cools down, prepare the dressing by pouring the olive oil in a small mixing bowl. Gradually add the lemon juice while vigorously whisking.
6. Whisk in the garlic, mustard, sweetener, pepper, and salt, set aside.
7. In a separate medium mixing bowl, combine the chilled cauliflower, peas, chives, almonds, and red onions, add dressing and stir to mix.
8. Transfer to an airtight container and refrigerate for a few hours until it's time to serve.

Macros Per Serving ¼ cup – Calories: 212 |Total Fat: 20g |Protein: 4g |**Net Carbs: 4g**

Sweet and Spicy Brussels Sprouts

Bursting with flavor, this sweet and spicy Brussels sprouts recipe will make the perfect side for a low carb main dish!

Prep Time: 10 Minutes
Cook Time: 10 Minutes
Total Time: 20 Minutes
Serves: 4

Ingredients:
- 2 Tbsp. sesame seed oil
- 1 Tbsp. soy sauce
- 1 Tbsp. sriracha
- 1.5 Tbsp. Sukrin Gold Syrup
- ¼ tsp. black pepper
- 1 lb. Brussels sprouts
- Sesame seeds
- Green onion
- Pink Himalayan sea salt

Directions:
1. Prepare the sweet and sour sauce by whisking together the sesame seed oil, soy sauce, sriracha, syrup and pepper, set aside.
2. Trim and quarter the Brussels sprouts and allow them to cook for about 5 minutes on each side in a large wok, cook on their flat sides for a few minutes before tossing them.
3. In the last 2 minutes of cooking, pour the sauce in and toss to coat thoroughly.
4. Season with salt to taste.
5. Sprinkle with sesame seeds and green onion.
6. Serve!

Macros Per Serving – Calories: 110 |Total Fat: 7g |Protein: 4g |**Net Carbs: 7.5g**

Mediterranean Pasta

Made with tomatoes, artichokes, garlic, and lemon, this healthy pasta recipe is easy to make and features bright flavors!

Prep Time: 5 Minutes
Cook Time: 3 Minutes
Total Time: 8 Minutes
Serves: 4

Ingredients:

- 2 large zucchini, spiral sliced
- 1 cup spinach, packed
- 2 Tbsp. olive oil
- 2 Tbsp. butter
- 5 cloves garlic, minced
- Sea salt and black pepper, to taste
- ¼ cup sun-dried tomatoes
- 2 Tbsp. capers
- 2 Tbsp. Italian flat leaf parsley, chopped
- 10 kalamata olives, halved
- ¼ cup Parmesan cheese, shredded
- ¼ cup feta cheese, crumbled

Directions:

1. In a large sauté pan over medium heat, add in the olive oil, zucchini, spinach, butter, garlic, sea salt and black pepper.
2. Sauté until zucchini is tender and spinach is wilted, drain the excess liquid.
3. Add in the sun-dried tomatoes, capers, parsley, and kalamata olives, mix in and sauté for 2 to 3 minutes.
4. Remove the pan from heat and toss with Parmesan and feta cheeses.
5. Serve!

Macros Per Serving – Calories: 231 |Total Fat: 20g |Protein: 6.5g |**Net Carbs: 6.5g**

Roasted Vegetable Masala

Easy main dish of vegetables features a delicious mixed of cauliflower, green beans and mushrooms roasted in a flavorful Indian spiced tomato sauce.

Prep Time: 10 Minutes
Cook Time: 20 Minutes
Total Time: 30 Minutes
Serves: 4

Ingredients:

Vegetables:

- 8 oz. Cauliflower, ½ a medium - large head
- 6 oz. green beans, sliced
- 4 oz. whole mushrooms, quartered

Masala:

- ½ cup tomato puree
- 2 Tbsp. olive oil, ghee, or melted butter
- 2 tsp. fresh ginger, minced
- 1 clove garlic, minced
- ½ tsp. chile powder (pure ground chiles)
- ¼ tsp. garam masala or sub with 1 part cumin and ¼ allspice
- ¼ tsp. turmeric
- Salt, to taste
- Pepper, to taste

Garnish

- Green onion, sliced
- Cilantro, chopped
- Siracha, optional

Directions:

1. Preheat oven to 400 degrees F or toaster oven to 375 degrees F.
2. Place rack to middle position, then cover a sheet pan in foil.
3. In a medium bowl, add the tomato puree, spices, minced garlic and ginger, stir in the liquid ghee or oil.
4. Add the cauliflower, green beans and mushrooms, stir to coat.
5. Spread the vegetables into a single layer on the prepared sheet pan and season with the salt and pepper.
6. Roast for 20 minutes or until the veggies are cooked well.
7. Garnish with green onion and cilantro.
8. Serve!

Macros Per Serving – Calories: 105 |Total Fat: 7g |Protein: 3g |**Net Carbs: 6g**

43647129R00064

Made in the USA
Middletown, DE
26 April 2019